Artificial Intelligence and its Applications

Artificial Intelligence and its Applications

Ivan Stanimirović, Olivera M. Stanimirović

ARCLER PRESS

www.arclerpress.com

Artificial Intelligence and its Applications

Ivan Stanimirović, Olivera M. Stanimirović

Arcler Press
224 Shoreacres Road
Burlington, ON L7L 2H2
Canada
www.arclerpress.com
Email: orders@arclereducation.com

ISBN: 978-1-77407-688-0 (Hardcover)

ABOUT THE AUTHORS

Ivan Stanimirovic gained his PhD from University of Niš, Serbia in 2013. His work spans from multi-objective optimization methods to applications of generalized matrix inverses in areas such as image processing and computer graphics and visualisations. He is currently working as an Assistant professor at Faculty of Sciences and Mathematics at University of Niš on computing generalized matrix inverses and its applications.

Olivera M. Stanimirović is currently with the Faculty of Sciences and Mathematics at University of Nis with a degree in mathematics and computer science. After her master's studies, she enrolled in doctoral studies at the Department of Mathematics in Nis as well. She participated in several international congresses, where she published her papers in optimization and applied mathematics.

TABLE OF CONTENTS

GLOSSARY

A

Aggregate: It is a table or structure that contains pre-calculated data for a cube. Support fast and efficient multidimensional tables.

D

Database (BD): Set of non-redundant data stored on a data carrier, organized independently of its use and accessible simultaneously by different users and applications. The difference from a BD respect to another data storage system is that they are stored in the database so that they meet three basic requirements: no redundancy, independence, and competition.

C

Client/Server: Information systems architecture in which application processes are divided into components that can run on different machines. Mode operation of an application in which two types of processes differ and its support is assigned to different platforms.

Coding: Transformation of a message in encrypted form, i.e., the specification for assigning unique characters of a repertoire (alphabet character set) to another repertoire. Converting an analog value into a digital signal by a preset code.

Cube: It is the central object data contains information on a multidimensional structure. Each cube is defined by a set of dimensions and measures.

D

Data dictionary: logical description of the data to the user. Gather information about the data stored in the database (descriptions, meaning, structures, safety considerations, editing, and application usage, etc.).

Data directory: It is a sub-management system database describing where and how data is stored in the database (access mode and physical characteristics thereof).

Datamart: It is a data structure that is optimized for access. It is designed to facilitate end-user access. It supports analysis applications used by multiple users.

Deviation detection: Typically, for detecting a deviation in large databases external explicit information data and integrity constraints or predefined models used. In a linear method, by contrast, the problem is approached from within the data, using the implicit data redundancy. Here is a familiar mechanism is simulated humans: after seeing a series of similar data, an element that disturbs the series is considered an exception.

Dimension: It is a tribute structure or a bucket that is organized by category hierarchies or levels describing data in the fact table. These categories describe a set of members which is based on the analysis. For example, a geographical dimension includes levels of countries, regions, states or provinces, and cities.

Drill-down (Start at the highest level and down to detail level to level): Obtaining more detailed information on a set in which you are working information. Example: If you are looking for assets, get all asset accounts.

E

Extranet: It is a service-oriented communication centered on the format of web systems, operating on the internet public. Example: A house sales of various products, implement a system offers, consult catalogs, databanks, and purchasing their preferred customers.

F

Fact table: It contains the key indicators identified during the analysis process and containing a combination of objects and time information.

Fact: It represents a row in a fact table in the information storage. It contains one or more numerical values that measure an event.

I

Inconsistency: The contents of a database are inconsistent if two data that should be equal are not. For example, an employee appears in a table as active, and in another, as retired.

Integrity: Safety condition ensures that the information is amended, including its creation and deletion, only by authorized personnel.

Internet: Term used to refer to the largest network in the world, connecting thousands of networks worldwide. It is creating a culture based on simplicity, research, and standardization based on real-life applications, it is changing the way of seeing and doing many of the tasks. Much of the technology in networks is coming from the internet community.

Intranet: It is a communication service corporate information systems oriented staff, the format of web systems, operating on the Internet.

M

Mapping: Data set.

List of data or objects, as they are currently stored in memory or on disk.

Transfer a set of objects from one place to another. For example, the program modules on the disk are projected ("mapped") in memory. A graphic memory image is projected on the screen.

Connect a set of objects with another. For example, a structure of the logical database is projected on the physical database.

P

Predictive modeling (artificial intelligence (AI)): Predictive modeling tools allow complex relationships or patterns from a data file. One of the main differences between statistical models and artificial intelligence models is how to measure their errors. The first measure the relative error as the model fits the data, while the second, measuring the error in the still invisible data (predictive error).

Statistical models have difficulty in giving conflicting or messy data, i.e., the data must be clean and should be consistent correlations. Conversely, artificial intelligence tools seek to generalize relationships to provide the most likely outcome. Abductive modeling (an argument that the major premise is obvious and less likely but more credible than the conclusion) uses polynomial functions to describe relationships within the data. This methodology provides an input variable to be weighted more than once. Further, only terms included that significantly contribute to performance.

Predictive models can be used to support the decision or making subroutines to develop predictive applications to customers. The capabilities of predictive models can be improved if the data files are enhanced with many input variables as possible.

M

Measure: It is a quantitative numerical column in the fact table. Usually, it represents the values to be analyzed.

Metadata: It is the result of modeling data. When data is stored in a tool or in a repository.

O

OLAP (Online analytical process): It is a process management database designed for decision support assistance, using tools that facilitate analysis of dimensional structures business information. A typical OLAP database provides consolidated, stored consistent data and historical data in read-only format.

OLTP (Online transactional process): It is a management system database that represents the state of a particular business at a specific point in time. An OLTP system has a large number of concurrent users adding and modifying data.

R

Record: Rating that is given to a group of customers/products that measures the propensity for purchases, sales, retirement, arrivals, etc.

Redundancy: Repeating the same data in multiple places.

Repository: Central database tools development aid. The repository broadens the concept of the data dictionary to include all information that is generated throughout the lifecycle of the system, such as components analysis and design (data flow diagram, entity-relationship diagrams, schematics databases, screen layouts, etc.), program structures, algorithms, etc. In some references, it is called an information resource dictionary.

M

Management system database: Software that controls the organization, storage, retrieval, security, and integrity of data in a database. Accepts requests for data from an application program and instructs the operating system to transfer the appropriate data. When a management system database, DBMS, (in English DBMS), information systems more easily can be changed as requirements change the organization is used. New categories of data can be added to the database without damaging the existing system.

S

Software: They are the intangibles applications developed in a programming language to solve a specific need implemented through a computer.

SQL (Structured query language): Standardized query language for relational databases. SQL is a high-level language, not procedural, standardized, which allows the query and update data from relational databases. It has become the standard for accessing relational databases. SQL provides a data definition language and data manipulation language. It also includes an interface that allows access and manipulation of the database to end-users.

System information (SI): Set of physical, logical elements, communication, data, and personnel, interrelated allow storage, transmission, and processing of information.

T

Terabyte (TB): Unit of measure equal to 1024 GB (Gigabytes).

Teradata: Management system relational database (RDBMS) Teradata is parallel relational database support powerful decisions for information storage. Teradata also provides client connectivity open to virtually all operating systems.

LIST OF FIGURES

LIST OF ABBREVIATIONS

ACN	attentional connectionist network
AI	artificial intelligence
ALICE	artificial linguistic internet computer entity
ANN	artificial neural networks
ANS	artificial neural systems
BLOBs	binary large objects
CORBA	broker architecture common object
CSCW	computer-supported collaborative work
DARPA	projects agency defense advanced research
DBMSs	database management systems
DCE	distributed computing environments
DSS	decision support systems
DWA	data warehouse application
EIS	executive information systems
FGCP	fifth generation computer project
GIS	geo-referential information systems
GPS	general problem solver
GUI	graphical user interface
HOAP	hybrid online analytical processing
INN	intelligent negotiation neural network
IS	information system
IS	intelligent systems
ISI	Institute of Scientific Information
IS–	International Organization for Standardization
JCR	Journal of Citation Report
LAN	local area network
LISA	Library and Information Science Database of Abstracts

MDDBs	multidimensional databases
MIS	management information systems
MOAP	multidimensional online analytical processing
MPP	massively parallel processing
NUMA	non-uniform memory access
OA	office systems
OLAP	online analytical process
OLAP	online analytical processing
RDBMS	relational DBMS
RUR	robots universal Rossum
SBS	systems business simulation
SIE	executive information system
SMP	symmetric multiprocessing
SOM	self-organizing map
SPD	spectral polarization difference
SQL	structured query language
TB	terabyte
TPM	topology-preserving map
VT	threshold voltage

PREFACE

Since the dawn of the information era, organizations have used data from operational systems to meet their information needs. Some provide direct access to the information within operational applications. Others have extracted the data from their operational databases to be combined in various unstructured ways, in an attempt to assist users in their information needs.

In this book, the changes to the world caused by the use of artificial intelligence *(*AI*)* and machine learning are investigated. It investigates the impact of the use of AI in everyday life, emphasizing technologies such as AI, machine learning, and deep learning. In recent years, advances in these areas have influenced considerably the technology as we know it, opening doors to new possibilities that once seemed unimaginable.

The brain is the most amazing organ in the human body. It sets the way we perceive the images, sounds, smells, tastes, and touch. It allows us to store memories, emotions, and even dream experience. Without it, we would be primitive organisms, incapable of anything but the simplest of reflexes. The brain is ultimately, what makes us intelligent. For decades, we have dreamed of building intelligent machines with brains like ours; robotic assistants to clean our homes, cars that drive themselves, microscopes automatically detect diseases. But, building these artificially intelligent machines requires us to solve some of the most complex computational problems we've had; problems that our brains can now be solved in a fraction of seconds. How to attack and solve these problems in the field of study of AI.

It is a concrete and easily verifiable fact that we are in the context of globalization and the revolution in information and communications technology, also called the "fourth industrial revolution." And therefore, the role of AI is nowadays something very important, because it is generating qualitative changes in our way of "doing" traditional and address these changes, under no circumstances can we remain indifferent, as this simply and would simply wallow in the worst setbacks.

The choice of this topic comes from a growing curiosity about these technologies. The advancement of technology, its uses and how they influence, on people have generated a great impact on today's society. This book intends to expand our knowledge on the subject and better understand the current state of the art in this field. It is something we have to be aware of, since it is increasingly present in our lives. We must understand the new technologies in order to use them correctly and optimize them in the future. The problem that certain jobs can be replaced by machines generates a change in the way of human thinking and doing, which must adopt these technologies and trained to use them. Man must evolve, to adapt to a world where jobs will require other approaches. AI and its branches have helped people automate everyday work tasks because of its potential which is able to replace certain work done by humans generating a change in the way of doing things.

CHAPTER 1

Introduction

CONTENTS

The study of intelligence is as old as civilization itself. The ability of the human brain to think for himself and to solve both simple and complex problems showing minimal effort has certainly been of great interest to scientists and philosophers, in order to discover and understand how this happens.

Some of the known definitions of intelligence are that of John McCarthy who says that intelligence is "the ability of humans to adapt effectively to changing circumstances by using information about those changes." This is what led to the desire to artificially simulate this behavior; this is where the study of artificial intelligence (AI) begins, a term that was formally coined in 1956 during the conference month in England, showing that AI is much more complex than we imagined in principle.

AI definitely arises from the influential work by Alan Turing, a British mathematician, where a new discipline of information science opens. While the fundamental ideas date back to the logic and algorithms of ancient Greece and mathematics from the Arabs, several centuries before Christ, the concept of getting artificial reasoning appears in the fourteenth century. In the late nineteenth century, formal logic powerful enough is obtained, along with machines capable of using such logic and solution algorithms.

AI was officially "born" in 1943 when Warren McCulloch and Walter Pitts proposed a neuron model of the human and animal brain. These abstract nerve neurons provided a symbolic representation of brain activity. Later, Norbert Wiener developed these ideas with others within the same field, within the field called "cybernetics." McCulloch formalized it and postulated that:

—"The brain is an intelligent problem solver, so that we must imitate the brain."

But we must consider the enormous complexity of it and the fact this is virtually impossible, not to mention the hardware or software era were up for similar projects.

He began to consider human thought as a simple coordination of tasks related to each other by symbols. It would lead to the realization of what they regarded as the fundamentals of intelligent problem solving, but it was still difficult without starting, joining together these simple activities. It was in the 50s when the scientists managed to make a system that had some success; it was called the Rosenblatt's Perceptron. This was a visual pattern recognition system in which efforts were associated so that they could resolve a range of problems, but these energies were diluted immediately.

It was in the 1960s when Alan Newell and Herbert Simon, who work proving theorems and computer chess manage to create a program called GPS (general problem solver: general troubleshooter). This was a system in which the user-defined environment based on a series of objects and operators could be applied on them. This program was able to work with the towers of Hanoi as well as crypto-arithmetical and other similar problems, operating, of course, with formalized microcosm representing the parameters within which problems could be solved. We could not make the GPS able to solve problems in the real world, or make important decisions.

In the 1970s, a team of researchers led by Edward Feigenbaum began to develop a project to solve problems of everyday life and to focus on more concrete problems. This is how the expert system was born. The first expert system was the Dendral called a mass spectrogram interpreter built in 1967, but the most influential prove to be the Mycin from 1974. The Mycin was able to diagnose blood disorders and prescribe the appropriate medication, an achievement in that time that was even used in hospitals (as Puff, Mycin variant commonly used in the Pacific Medical Center in San Francisco, USA).

Already in the 1980s, special languages were developed for use with artificial, such as LISP or prolog intelligence. It is at this time when more sophisticated expert systems are developed, for example, the EURISKO. This program improves your own body heuristic rules automatically, by induction.

In 1987, Martin Fischles and Oscar Firschein described the attributes of an intelligent agent. When trying to describe a larger area (not only communication) attributes of an intelligent agent, the AI has expanded into many areas that have created huge and differentiated branches of research. The attributes of intelligent agents are:

- It has mental attitudes such as beliefs and intentions.
- Has the ability to gain knowledge, i.e. to learn.
- It is able to solve problems, including partitioning complex problems into simpler ones.

- It understands. It has the ability to create sense, if possible, to ambiguous or contradictory ideas.
- It plans, predicts consequences, evaluates alternatives (like chess games).
- It knows the limits of its own abilities and knowledge.
- It may be original, even creating new concepts or ideas, and even using analogies.
- It is able to generalize.
- It can perceive and model the outside world.
- It can understand and use language and symbols.

We can then say that the AI has human characteristics such as learning, adaptation, reasoning, self-correction, implicit improvement, and modular perception of the world. Thus, we can talk not only an objective but many, depending on the viewpoint or utility that can be found in the AI.

In 1990, intelligent agents arise. The artificial linguistic internet computer entity (ALICE) program won the award for most human Loebner Chatbot in 2000, 2001, and 2004, and in 2007, the Hal assistant program won the award.

Today it is so far from meeting the famous Turing test when formulated as:

— "The AI will be truly intelligent if we are not able to distinguish between a human and a computer program in a blind conversation."

Anecdotally, many AI researchers argue that "Intelligence is a program capable of being executed independently of the machine you run it, or computer brain"

Suzette in 2010 the program won the Loebner Prize. Some programs are free AI Dr. Abuse, Alice, Paula SG, virtual woman millennium.

AI is a science with a wide field of study devoted to the study of the human brain and intelligence. In order to model mathematically different logic and processes help facilitate and automate problems in different areas of knowledge. Its applications are varied and are present in many areas where their model is the human being, and there are q take into account the different problems that arise.

Heman has tried to constantly explain the human brain, as the human being is able to perceive, understand, analyze, and manipulate a whole world of mysteries. AI attempts to build, not only to comprise an intelligent entity (Stuart and Peter, 2004). Being one of the most recent sciences, he began studying it soon after the Second World War. AI is born in this year of Dartmouth, in Hanover a meeting in which they participated in what later would be the main researchers in the area, a proposal that appears for the first time the term "AI" was written.

AI is the branch of science studying software and hardware necessary to simulate the behavior and compression of the human brain. AI has several objectives among which they can discuss and explain the need to create machines with AI that are able to discern, think, and reason in the way that humans make, simulating their feelings and are able to be aware. Here comes many great trouble defining intelligence in various ways, analyzing from many points of view, one of the problems that are difficult to simulate is the awareness.

AI, an area which began with Marvin Minsky in 1956, is closely linked to computers and other areas of computer knowledge, it aims to have the ability to create intelligent machines and distinguishes two types of intelligence, natural, and artificial (Barba, 2001).

During the beginning of AI, there was a thrill around it with the intention of advancing equal to that of AI people, getting a computable to feel, reason, and be on your own ratio. Due to the technology that already existed at the time of software and hardware, it was thought it would be very easy to achieve this, and to express this phenomenon computationally, this current investigation is known as strong AI. AI had started with very ambitious goals, which in the nineties had a setback because the practical results did not support the theoretical, in many cases, all the ideas and goals had become mere speculation. Today, we have managed to simulate various situations with developing hardware and software, as decision making in commercial matters. But scientists have not achieved after fifty years of AI, to simulate that are simple to humans, such as intuition and awareness is still no progress today is still debating whether it is possible to create a computer with reasoning behaviors and consciousness.

1.1. ARTIFICIAL NEURAL NETWORKS (ANN)

Neural networks have been studied almost since the beginning of the computer age. At first, neural network, research was motivated by biology. But models of developed neural networks were too weak to solve complex processing tasks information that can be found in many industrial applications.

New innovations in the 80s led to the emergence of more powerful models of neural networks. Many scientific studies have attempted to successfully demonstrate the concepts and benefits of various sectors of industrial applications. Consequently, the industry considered neural networks as a useful tool.

Today, neural networks are popular and are applied in various industry sectors. In the past, he had exaggerated claims about the ability of neural networks. But researchers and users worked on an improved understanding of the models and reporting of the advantages and disadvantages in different industrial sectors. Now the field of neural networks is more realistic and is following the right track.

Realistic expectations and actual experiences have succeeded in reducing the risk of failures and bad reputations generated by them. If this knowledge can be combined with the experience in industrial automation applications, they can achieve the level of performance capabilities of neural networks.

In our nervous system, cells called neurons are a processing unit that receives an electrical stimulus from other neurons mainly through its dendritic tree. The electrical stimulus received by passing a certain threshold causes the neuron, in turn, to send an electrical signal through its axon to other successive neurons. The strength of the interconnection between neurons in the network, enables the detection of complex patterns.

When the dendritic tree receives electrical pulses on a threshold voltage (TV), the specific neuron sends an electrical signal through the axon to axon terminals. In those terminal axon terminals are connected (via synapses) to other neurons. Axon terminals can be connected through synapses to different parts of the neuron but typically considered an only connection to other dendrites. Depending neurotransmitter induced postsynaptic potential terminal (dendrite) can be positive (excited) or negative (inhibitory).

Neurons have an activation time of the order of nanoseconds to milliseconds compared to computer hardware. The human brain has about 1011 neurons with an average of 104 connections each. All input signals from other neurons are added spatiotemporal manner by the neuron.

When the neuron is stimulated past a TV is depolarized (TDP) membrane and pumps sodium-potassium stop to act, the membrane changes to state and become more permeable to the positive ion of Na+ to enter the neuron changes the potential across the neuronal membrane to positive (+ 40mV).

Then there is a refractory period (TR) of ~ 1ms in which Na + channels are closed, the membrane is again permeable to K +, pumps are activated and the neuron reaches its initial voltage through exhaust K + in this period neuron is not susceptible to synaptic stimuli.

McCulloch and Pitts (1943) developed the original model of a neuron is included different inputs (x), weights for those inputs (w), a nonlinear function (f) transfer and output (O).

The neural net is modeled as a network with weights (synaptic connections) from nodes j to node i, w_{ij} (Figure 1.1). Neuron net input is:

$$S_i = \sum_j w_{ij} x_j$$

Output function f is the sign function given as:

$$O_i = \begin{cases} -1 \text{ if } S_i < \Theta_i \\ 1 \text{ if } S_i \geq \Theta_i \end{cases}$$

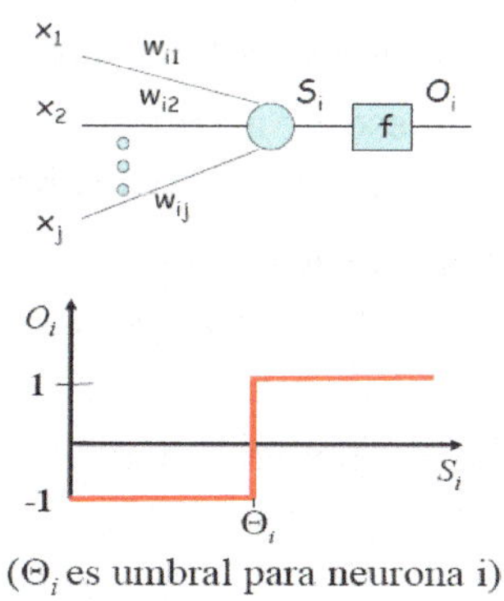

Figure 1.1. Neuron model.

McCullough and Pitts (1943) showed that this model could calculate logical functions to build finite state machines that can build logic gates (AND, OR, NOT). These gates can calculate any logic function using a network of two AND-OR levels. Also, it is called a layer perceptron (Figure 1.2).

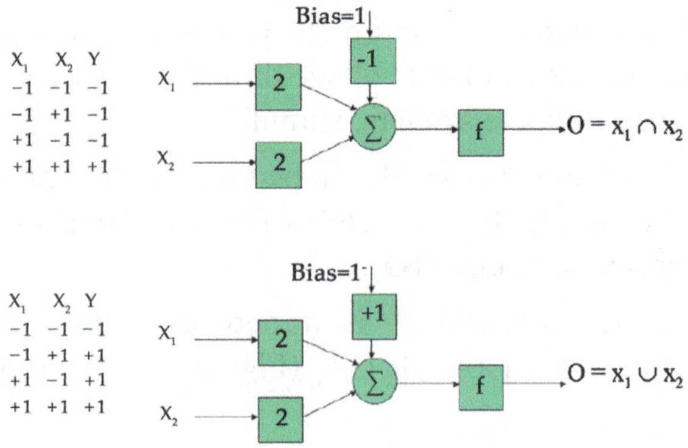

Figure 1.2. Neuronal computation.

ANNs are a paradigm for computation and detection patterns based on parallel interconnections of artificial neurons.

ANNs are based on complex nervous systems of animals and humans with its large number of interconnections and parallelism models.

Intelligent behaviors of these are an emergent property of a large number of units not a result of symbolic rules or algorithms.

The features previously exposed neurons are duplicated to create artificial neural networks (ANN) that have similar capabilities to process information in parallel.

Some capabilities of neural networks are:

1. Learning;
2. Classification;
3. Information storage;
4. Inter-polarization;
5. Adaptation.

ANN recreate or model the characteristics of neurons already mentioned in computer software and hardware systems. They are using groups of many artificial neurons (McCulloch-Pitts as neuron or MP). Use principles of collective and decentralized computing (parallel), they are able to learn.

Robust and resistant to failures of individual neurons operations, the network makes associations automatically, the network creates the "program" to adjust the weights while learning to operate require synchronized or signals enter simultaneously to all neurons in the same level (not using biological spatiotemporal sum).

The model of a neural network with multiple layers different from those we have seen so far including neurons in layers, a hidden layer means that it is not visible either the input or the output, a perceptron two layers can discern, polygonal regions, one of three or more layers can discern arbitrary regions (multi-layer perceptron or MLP).

These ANN have the ability to separate inputs in multiple linear functions and thus can detect more complex networks of a linear function as seen above patterns (Figure 1.3).

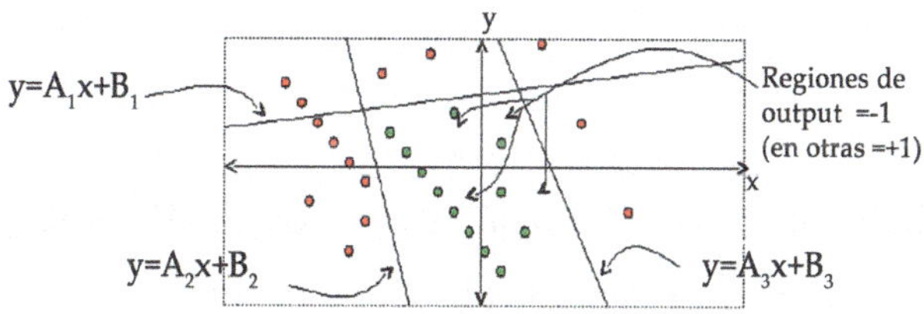

Figure 1.3. Neural network model multilayered.

Here is an example of a neural multilayer network is able to solve the problem of the XOR, the values on the lines indicate weights and circles indicate thresholds (thresholds), the nonlinear function is a step function with values of 1 if the threshold exceeded and the 0 if the threshold is not exceeded (Figure 1.4).

X_1	X_2	Y
0	0	0
0	1	1
1	0	1
1	1	0

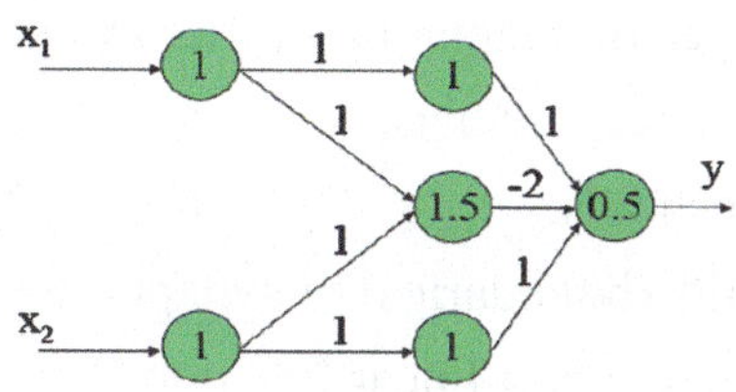

Figure 1.4. Example of XOR.

Typical nonlinear functions (f) used in neural networks include: sigmoid hard limiting (step function), and ramp, the sigmoid f (s) are (Figure 1.5):

- Monotonic (seamless);
- Bounded (limited);
- Have simple derivatives f '(s) = kf (s) [1–f (s)];

- Nonlinear.

Hard limiting and ramps are:

- Not monotonic (discontinuities);
- No simple derivatives;
- Linear (within limits areas).

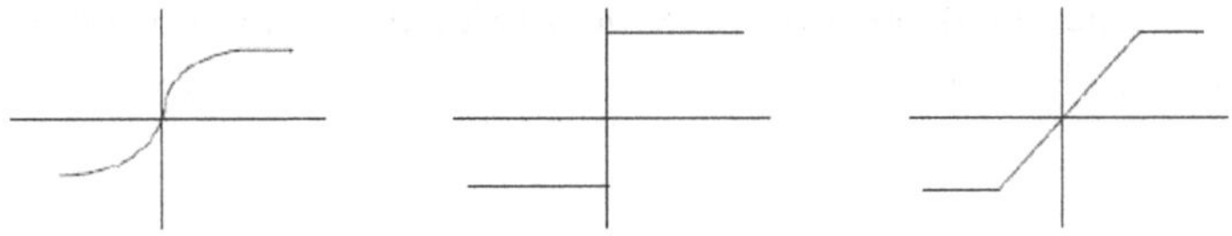

Figure 1.5. Nonlinear functions.

The following parameters should be considered (Figures 1.6 and 1.7):

- Size: number of neurons to solve a problem;
- Type or paradigm: number of hidden layers, the number of neurons in each layer;
- Learning algorithm;
- Number of iterations during learning;
- Number of calculations per iteration;
- Speed to recognize a pattern;
- Ability to recognize different patterns;
- Degree of adaptability (after training);
- If you require bias;
- Thresholds;
- Limits (boundaries) of synaptic weights;
- Selecting non-linear function (f);
- Network immunity necessary noise;
- Final values of the weights (final program) network.

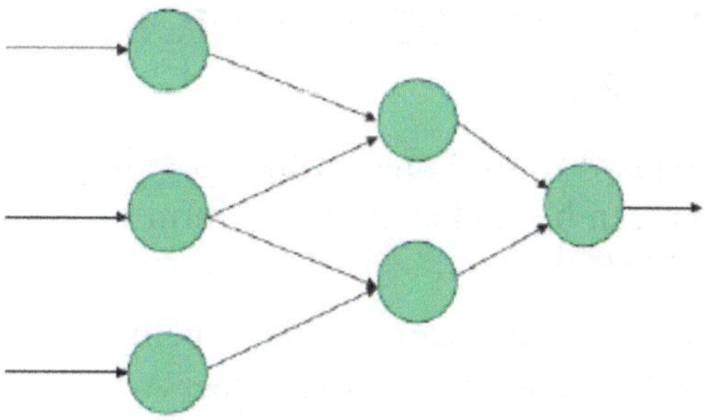

Figure 1.6. Multilayer feedforward with a hidden layer.

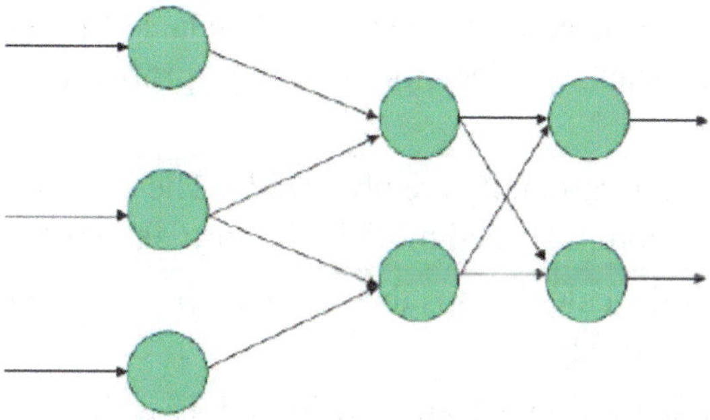

Figure 1.7. Multilayer feedforward with hidden and competitive/cooperative layers.

Bilayer feedforward/backward without hidden layers (Figure 1.8):

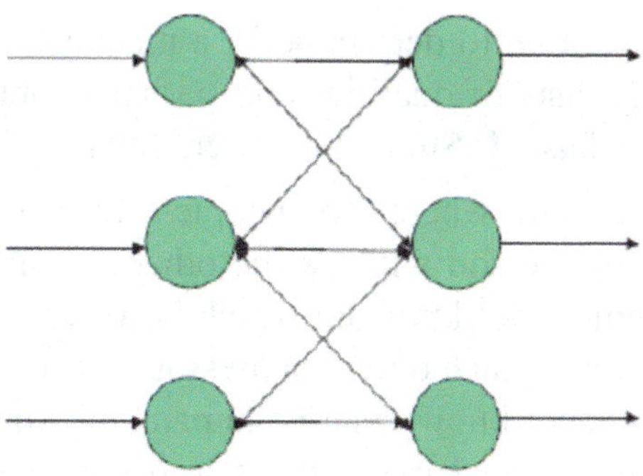

Figure 1.8. Bilayer feedforward/backward without hidden layers.

1.2. THE DEFINITION OF ARTIFICIAL INTELLIGENCE (AI)

AI may have several ways to define it; the most important are the mental processes and what can be said as the ideal form of intelligence reasoning (Stuart and Peter, 2004).

"The objective of this science is to build computer models, defined as capable of intelligent behavior, in which engineers work specialist computing, neurosciences, and science conduct" (Barba, 2001). Systems that think like humans are observed: "The exciting new effort to make computers think. Machines with minds in the broadest literal sense" (Haugeland, 1985).

"The automation is activities that we associate with thought processes, human activities such as decision making, problem-solving, learning" (Bellman, 1978).

Systems thinking rationally are observed: "The study of mental faculties through the use of computerized models" (Charniak and McDermott, 1985).

"The study of the calculations that makes it possible to perceive, reason, and act" (Winston, 1992).

Systems that act rationally are considered as well: "The computational intelligence is the study of design intelligent agents "(Poole et al., 1998).

There exist several methods to determine if a machine is intelligent. These are the famous Turing test, the Chinese room, and other algorithms.

1.2.1. The Turing Test

In Alan Turing's invention to determine if, a machine is intelligent or not, this test avoids large lists of qualities and perhaps controversial to define whether the machine has AI (Stuart and Peter, 2004).

Turing test is a game where two people and a machine in different rooms will judge. One person will ask the other two in order to recognize the human and machine, not knowing which is which and only with labels X, Y will be connected to each other via messages. If the judge after having the conversation does not know what is human and what is a machine, the machine passed the test of Turing and it is declared intelligent (Turing, 1950).

1.2.2. The Chinese Room by J. Searle

There is an experiment used to challenge the validity of the Turing test, is known as the Chinese room was proposed by John Searle. The experiment tries to explain that a machine can perform intelligent actions, but at the same time the machine is not aware of his act of intelligence, i.e., not able to discern or understand the machine is doing, just follow an algorithm designed for such function (Penrose, 1991). The experiment proposes a machine which is isolated exterior. The machine does not know the language, but is within reach of dictionary and instructions that will tell you the rules of language, in this way and thanks to the manuals. Computer will be able to convince the person on the outside that it knows the native language, although we have never spoken or read this language (Penrose, 1991). Searle raises the following questions:

1. "How can you respond if you do not understand the Chinese language?
2. Did the instructional know Chinese?
3. Can you consider all the system room as a system that understands Chinese? "(Penrose, 1991).

Then an operation or activity is carried out without understanding being made only by following the algorithm, the same machine follows the same algorithm or program for which it was designed uncomprehending (Searle, 1980a). Accordingly this effect, it is only a simulation of what is the human mind, as symbols that manipulate have no meaning for the machine cannot be considered really smart, so much that it seems (Searle, 1980a).

1.2.3. Algorithms

AI within the algorithm is defined as a set of rules or finite and predetermined processes, designed to obtain a satisfactory result. They are operations logic seeking to obtain an output or result from stimulation or input. The algorithms can be applied to many areas efficient manner.

1.3. TYPES OF ARTIFICIAL INTELLIGENCE (AI)

- ***Weak Artificial Intelligence (AI):*** Supporters of weak AI stipulate that a machine can never be conscious and will never have a natural intelligence and pure reasoning, supporters of weak AI are based on computers and machines can only pretend to reason and act intelligently

- ***Strong Artificial Intelligence (AI):*** Strong AI considers that a computer can have a mind and mental states, and therefore can build a computer that contains all the capabilities of a human mind, being able to reason, imagine, create, design, and do other things that yet are only utopias

1.4. APPLICATIONS OF ARTIFICIAL INTELLIGENCE (AI)

1. ***Branches of Artificial Intelligence (AI):*** The AI systems can be classified into three basic categories: expert systems (Knowledge-based), natural language systems and systems of language natural systems perception for vision, speech, and touch (Wendy, 1985).

- ***Expert Systems*****:** Are programs that are using processes of reasoning to solve problems in specific fields of knowledge, help solve problems based on human experimental knowledge and skills (Wendy, 1985). That is, they are programs that help solve problems that normally do human experts.
- ***The Natural Language Systems*****:** These systems comprise and expressed in the language human, thus giving the information in a language that anyone can understand without having to learn a computer language, it is very commonly used in base data (Wendy, 1985).
- ***Systems for Visual, Audible, and Tactile Perception*****:** This is still one of the most limited with respect to their abilities fields are used in certain conditions (Wendy, 1985).

2. ***Artificial Neural Systems (ANS):*** The neural networks appear in order to help solve problems with conventional machines are almost impossible or too tedious to perform, to solve this problem several features will take the physiology brain as the basis for new models of prosecutions. These techniques have been called ANS or just networking neuronal (Skapura, 1996).

Neural networks are AI programs with the ability to simulate the learning functions of human beings. A network neuronal gets experience analysis automatic and systematic data provided to determine rules of behavior and thus make predictions of new cases (Luis, 2004).

3. ***Neurons and Synaptic Connections:*** Every neuron can have infinite enter called dendrites and has only an existing outlet, the axon; these can be connected to each other by synapses.

In this model is considered a neuron can be represented by a binary unit (Luis, 2004). One of the main features and one of the best neural networks is adaptive learning, this feature allows us to constantly change in order to adapt to new conditions job (Sotolongo et al, 2001).

4. ***AI in Robotics***: Robotics is the science multidisciplinary charge of designing and building machines (Roth et al, 1987). The word robot was first used by Karel Capek used in one of his works comes from the Czech word "Robota" meaning servitude or forced labor (De Santos et al, 2010).

Today the term applies to all robots powered and electronically controlled mechanical devices capable of performing discharge of machines, and assembly operations welding among others, this field is aimed at developing machines that know interact with the environment in which they operate (Roth et al, 1987).

AI comes into this field in order to create intelligent machines capable of performing calculations, think, reason, make judgments, and decisions (De Santos et al, 2010).

Not only that also our interest. It focuses on intelligent agents that manipulate the physical world, and a field of great interest is to apply ideas as planning or artificial (Roth et al, 1987) vision.

5. ***Artificial Life***: Artificial life is "the study of the facts systems the man that exhibit behaviors characteristic of natural living systems "according to Christopher Langton (Moriello, 2004).

The most important difference between these two branches that can be confusing and is a debate very intense in the forums of science among great scientists, it is its subject. VA studies the life and explores how to address the synthetic or construction of artificial systems displayed in living properties, which makes them suitable or improved for certain types of jobs or even prosthetic. In change, AI reduces its study and exploration of human intelligence in order to simulate a machine (Lazhoz-Beltra, 2004). The relationship between artificial life and AI is getting closer so experts predict that the future will converge, because biological life and intelligence are mutually dependent, the VA and AI exhibit codependence (Moriello, 2004) (Figure 1.9).

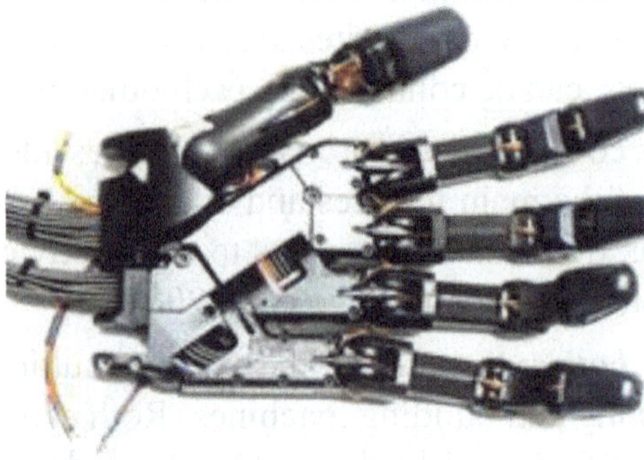

Figure 1.9. Prosthetic hand.

6. ***AI in Medicine***: The breakthrough of the media computer in recent years, sample the key role of computers in the medical field, a simple example is the engineering biomedical.

The development of different techniques applied to AI medicine represents a new perspective, which can reduce costs, weather, medical errors, and enhance the human resources in medical branches with higher requirements. The development of these areas would have a special appropriate assistance to the physician in decision making, future professionals in their practice and in the area of diagnosis from rare diseases or difficult to identify.

1.5. THE PROBLEMS OF ARTIFICIAL INTELLIGENCE (AI)

The experiences of human beings, are very difficult to translate into a symbolic language or a language that a machine can interpret and interact as they would a human being, such as the scent of a flower, the taste of a soup, a fabric texture, including the philosophers call this experience as qualia, qualia cannot be described, are unique experiences of human beings. For a machine, starts to seem more human should be able to understand these qualities, this science is facing a very complex wall, and that it may be impossible to achieve (Ferri, 2004).

Perhaps the AI this beyond our abilities or is only a matter of time, humans have always compared the brain with advances in technology and the mechanics. A strong critic of AI, Humbert compares with a metaphor that progress made in the field amount to a tree trying to reach the moon, still nobody knows whether they can solve these problems, AI has an uncertain future (Ferri, 2004).

AI is one of the areas that have more work because their fields are many and all have a lot to develop and research. AI seeks the model that has all the qualities and characteristics of a human being, from their ability to think, reason, and create the ability to solve problems of everyday life. It is very difficult to build a machine capable of having feelings, to imagine and discern like a human being. Some people think that this will not be achieved due to the high complexity and experiences impossible to place in a code machine language such as the qualia. This is an issue of great debate between defending and criticizing the AI, but you could see the human being and as a machine program. It can be argued that we are automated beings and created with the ability to develop thousands of algorithms that allow us to be and consider ourselves intelligent beings. Since we can consider that everything that makes our brain is based on electrical impulses, information receipted abroad by our senses of sight, smell, hear, touch, and taste, which reaches our brain as input and stimulation and that is where it is processed by neurons, which pass information to each other in order to command our body an adequate response to such stimulus.

Considering as an output, we can think of our brain as an integrated computer with a processor huge and able to expand and adapt to different needs, this brain encounter within a mechanical body, adapted, and designed to accomplish different tasks the main part or assign. Then we are a machine or are human beings, the possibilities are endless with the advancement of science and technology knows if it will remain a utopia AI or will become reality.

Current applications of AI leads us to obtain an automated world, in order to expedite the various processes and prevent human errors in each of them, in solving problems and making people's lives easier.

Within this book, we will:

- Investigate the use and applications of AI in everyday life.
- Explain the changes that AI-generated in the way of thinking and making people.
- Explain the impacts of using machines to perform human tasks.

1.6. BASIC NOTIONS AND NOTATIONS

Let us define key concepts that will later be used in this work. "It is called AI to the faculty of reasoning holds an agent who is not alive, as in the case of software which contains a robot, to quote one of the best-known examples, and which it was conferred by the design and development of various processes just gestated by humans."

Notably, in addition to the power to reason, these devices are able to develop many behaviors and human activities such as solving a given problem, playing sports, etc. This way you can understand that intelligences are autonomous systems: In short, autonomy means that an AI, already developed, does not need help from people. An example can be autonomous cars that do not need human help (to some extent). A more crudely, AI is nothing more than a series of algorithms: The most important part of AI is the algorithm. These are mathematical formulas and/or programming commands that inform an unintelligent about resolving problems with AI regular computers. Algorithms are rules that teach computers to work things out for themselves. Hence, the concept of machine learning (machine learning) is clear: It is generally acceptable to replace the term AI and machine learning. However, they are not the same, but are connected. "Machine learning is the process by which an AI uses algorithms to perform functions of AI. It is the result of applying rules to create results through an AI" Julian (2015) "key algorithms in the search for AI." They are not the same, but they are connected. "Machine learning is the process by which an AI uses algorithms to perform functions of AI. It is the result of applying rules to create results through an AI. "Julian (2015)" key algorithms in the search for AI. "They are not the same, but they are connected." Machine learning is the process by which an AI uses algorithms to perform functions of AI. It is the result of applying rules to create results through an AI. "Julian (2015)" key algorithms in the search for AI."

AI can be divided into several branches to be studied. It is true that there are similarities, but each is more specific or can be used for other tasks. Including AI can be divided into narrow (narrow) and strong (strong).

According to Ben Dickson (2017), the founder of TechTalks, "The AI strait is the only form of AI that humanity has achieved so far. This is the one that is good to perform a single task, such as playing chess or Go, make purchase suggestions, sales predictions and forecasts. Computer vision, the natural language processing still in the stage of close AI. Speech recognition and the image is a narrow AI, even if your progress seems fascinating.

General AI, also known as human-level AI and strong AI, is the kind of AI that can understand and reason their environment as would a human being.

John McCarthy coined the term "AI" in 1956, and defined it as "science and ingenuity of making intelligent machines, especially intelligent computer programs."

As in conventional computer science, AI we have a number of unique elements that characterize and differentiate. According to Nilsson (1971) are four basic pillars on which rest AI:

- Search required in all the states produced by the possible actions state;
- Genetic algorithms (analogous to the process of evolution of DNA strands);
- ANN (analogous to the physical functioning of the brain of animals and humans); and
- Reasoning by formal logic abstract one analogous to human thought.

Then we will make a brief description of previous research that contributed greatly to the field of AI as we know it today. One of the first philosophical reference points came courtesy of computer pioneer Alan Turing. In 1950, he first described what became known as "The Turing Test," in his essay "computing machinery and intelligence" and what he called "The imitation game," a test to measure when we can finally declare that machines can be intelligent.

His test was simple: if a judge cannot differentiate between a human and a machine (for example, through an interaction of one text with both), can the machine fool the judge into thinking it is he who is human? Amusedly at the time, Turing made a bold prediction about the future of computing, and calculated that by the end of the twentieth century, the test will have been approved. Sadly, his prediction was a bit premature, because as we begin to see a truly impressive AI now, in 2000 the technology was much more primitive.

One of the investigations which led to a great discovery to develop more powerful and capable minds was that of the neural network.

"Neural network" is the popular name that scientists give trial and error, the key concept that unlocks modern AI. Basically, when it comes to train an AI, the best way is to make the system guesses, receive feedback and guess again, constantly changing the odds to reach the correct answer.

What is quite surprising is that the first neural network was established in 1951. Called "SNARC" – computer analog reinforcement stochastic neural – was created by Marvin Minsky and Dean Edmonds and was not made of microchips and transistors, but pipe vacuum motors and clutches. Is the challenge for this machine? Helping a virtual rat to solve a puzzle maze. The system would send instructions to navigate through the maze and each time the effects of their actions would be fed back to the system; vacuum tubes would be used to store the results. This meant that the machine could learn and change the odds, thus increasing the chances of passing through the maze. It is essentially a very simple version of the same process that Google uses to identify objects in the photos today.

Another discovery which meant a breakthrough for AI was that of autonomous vehicles that did not require a driver.

When we think of cars without driver, we think of something like Google Waymo project, but surprisingly in 1995, Mercedes-Benz was able to drive a modified mostly autonomously from Munich to Copenhagen S Class.

Apparently, the car reached speeds up to 115 mph, and it was actually quite similar to the autonomous cars today as it was able to overtake and read traffic signs (Figure 1.10).[1]

Figure 1.10. Global robotic market (June 2015).

In the graph above it can be seen a prediction made by the BCG, A consulting firm recognized worldwide, where the growth of robotics and its possible impact on the professions analyzed.

The main social impact of AI probably replacing workers with machines, either in the productive process industries 4.0 or at the tip of the chain, such as customer service. Researchers at the University of Oxford (2013)

1 O'Malley, 2018 J World of tech

a global survey conducted by analyzing 702 occupations and automation opportunities for the next 20 years. A scale was considering the weaknesses of robots and what professions require a human being and not a machine, depending on the ability to develop creative solutions, social interactions, and negotiation skills. In the result of this research, the profession with a 99% probability of extinction is telemarketing. Other occupations that deserve mention are:

- Tax accountant, with 98.7% of chance to be automated.
- Credit analyst, 97.9%.
- Truck Driver 97.9%.
- Trade box retail 97.1%.
- Seller retail 92.3%.

All these activities have already begun testing robots, some showing operation with satisfactory results for the investing companies. According to a survey by McKinsey Global Institute, China is forecast to lose about 395 million jobs by machines in the next 3 years. Research suggests that in this same period, India should lose 235 million while the US will extinct 60 million jobs. On the other hand, specialists who advocate the use of AI argue that technology does not replace people, but increases their ability to do their job better by expanding their cognitive field. The truth is that professionals combine technological developments and are easy to act in line with robots; they have more opportunities to stay in the market. Concluding his analysis of Comstor's blog, the article entitled the social impact of the development of AI

In the short and medium-term, it is expected that AI brings with it efficiency and savings, not only in production and trade, but also in areas such as transport, healthcare, education, and agriculture, and, thanks to them, it can be avoided that humans are exposed to dangerous conditions such as, for example, cleaning of contaminated sites with toxic substances (Maradiaga, 2017) AI and its impact on society. Research is still required in the area, but it is undeniable that this sector has grown exorbitantly in the last 10 years.

In the near future, intelligent machines replace or enhance human capabilities in many areas previously considered strictly within the human domain. Such machines will affect the daily lives of people only forms in the history of mankind, and will change the shape of society as we know it now (Weizenbaum, 1972). Although many philosophers, science fiction writers, and others have speculated about other robots and AI-related products. For all we know, there has been little effort to examine the field of AI as a whole (in its relationship with society) in an organized manner.

1.7. ARTIFICIAL INTELLIGENCE (AI) IN A HISTORICAL CONTEXT

In this section, a brief summary of the history of AI will be presented, beginning with Alan Turing in 1950 to reach today.

Despite all the current hype, the AI is not a new field of study, but is based in the fifties. If we exclude the path of pure philosophical reasoning that goes from ancient Greek to Hobbes, Leibniz, and Pascal, AI, as we know it officially began in 1956 at Dartmouth College, where the most eminent experts gathered to exchange ideas about simulating intelligence. This happened only a few years after Asimov established his three laws of robotics, but more relevant after the famous article by Turing (1950), which first proposed the idea of a thinking machine and the most popular Turing test to assess whether such a machine shows, in fact, any intelligence (Corea, 2017).

From 1957 to 1974, the AI flourished. Computers could store more information and be faster, cheaper, and more accessible. Machine learning algorithms also improved and people familiar with the algorithms. First demonstrations as Newell and Simon's "GPS" and Joseph Weizenbaum's "ELIZA" showed promise towards the goals of problem-solving and interpretation of spoken language respectively. These successes convinced government agencies, such as project agency defense advanced research (DARPA), to fund research in various institutions AI. The government was particularly interested in a machine that could transcribe and translate the spoken language, as well as high data processing performance. Optimism was high and expectations were even higher.

In 1970, Marvin Minsky told life magazine, "within three to eight years we will have a machine with the general intelligence of an average human being." However, although the basic proof of principle was there, there was still a long way to go.

The ultimate goals of natural language processing, abstract thinking and self-recognition could be achieved (Marr, 2016) the ultimate goals of natural language processing, abstract thinking and self-recognition could be achieved (Marr, 2016) the ultimate goals of natural language processing, abstract thinking and self-recognition could be achieved.

After the initial fog of AI, a mountain of obstacles revealed. The biggest was the lack of computational power to do something substantial: computers simply could not store enough information or process it fast enough. To communicate, for example, one needs to know the meaning of many words and understand them in many combinations. Hans Moravec, a doctoral student at that time McCarthy said that "computers were still millions of times too weak to exhibit intelligence." As the patient decreased, also, it decreased funding, and research began to develop slowly over 10 years (Schultebrauks Lasse, 2017).

In the 1980s, the AI was rekindled by two sources: an expansion of the game of algorithmic tools and a boost of funds. John Hopfield and David Rumelhart popularized deep learning techniques or deep learning that allowed computers to learn using the experience. On the other hand, Edward Feigenbaum introduced expert systems that mimicked the decision-making process of a human expert. The program will ask an expert in a field how to respond in a given situation, and once this has been learned for virtually any situation, no experts could receive advice from the program.

Expert systems have been widely used in industries. The Japanese government-funded largely expert systems and related AI as part of its fifth-generation computer project (FGCP) ventures. From 1982 to 1990, invested $400 million in order to revolutionize computer processing, logic programming implement and improve AI. Unfortunately, most ambitious targets were not met. However, it could be argued that the indirect effects of FGCP inspired a generation of talented engineers and scientists. Anyway, FGCP funding ceased and AI fell outside the spotlight.

Ironically, in the absence of public funds and exaggerations, AI prospered. During the 1990s and 2000s, many of the historic goals of AI had been achieved. In 1997, the current world chess champion Gary Kasparov and Grandmaster were defeated by IBM's Deep Blue, a computer chess program. This highly publicized match was the first time that a reigning world chess champion lost to a computer and served as a major step towards making program artificially intelligent decisions. In the same year, the speech recognition software developed by dragon systems was implemented in Windows. This was another big step forward, but in the direction of stress interpretation of spoken language. It seemed there was a problem that machines could not handle. Even human emotion was a fair game as evidenced by Kismet, a robot developed by Cynthia Breazeal that could recognize and show emotions (Rockwell, 2017).

Now we live in the age of "big data," a time when we have the ability to collect vast amounts of information too heavy for a person to process. The application of AI in this regard has already been quite fruitful in various industries, such as technology, banking, marketing, and entertainment. We have seen that even if the algorithms do not improve much, big data and massive computing simply allow AI to learn through brute force (Marr, 2016).

So what awaits us in the future? In the immediate future, the AI language is seen as the next big thing. In fact, it is already underway. These days, machines are even calling people either to offer a product or service. One could imagine interacting with an expert system in a fluent conversation, or having a conversation in two different languages being translated in real-time. We can also expect to see cars without drivers on the road in the next twenty years (massively). A long-term goal is a general intelligence, which is a machine that surpasses human cognitive abilities in all tasks. This is in line with the sensitive robot we're used to seeing in movies. Although this is inconceivable that this will be achieved over the next 50 years. Even if the capacity is there, ethics serve as a strong barrier against. When that time (but even better before it reaches the time), we will have a serious conversation about politics and ethics of the machine (ironically, both issues mainly humans), but for now, let the AI constantly improve and not you go crazy in society.

This book is presenting an analysis of the interviews of the persons mentioned, in which they talked about the development and future of AI. In this paper, the two points on the themes respondents compared discussed AI itself, but more deeply the area of machine learning (machine learning). This is the branch of AI that has more impact. "Specifically an application is said to be learning machine does improve their performance on a task as it processes information. As you learn it gets better" (J. Grouville). According to our research objectives, as outlined in the introduction, we will make an analysis and comparison to determine if AI and its branches have helped people automate everyday tasks, because of their potential which is able to replace certain work done by humans generating a change in the way we do things and "is correct or not." In the interview, they discussed social, economic, and ethical as well as talk about both the past and future of AI.

1.8. MEANING OF AI

Intelligence from the psychological point of view is the cognitive ability of learning and relationship; bi-logical is the ability to adapt to new situations. Intelligence is linked to the ability to make the best choices and decisions when solving any kind of problem and depending on their attributes or processes there are various types of operational intelligence, biological intelligence or psychological intelligence.

AI or AI is one created by man and not by nature emulating their own intelligence through analysis of its mechanism and replaying it in machines. So you can define AI as the study of the creation and design of entities capable of thinking for themselves using as a paradigm of human intelligence.

AI brings together various fields such as robotics and expert systems and is examples of AI software able to respond to diagnostics, handwriting recognition, and speech patterns and are now routine in such fields as economics, medicine, engineering, military, and games strategy like chess among many other applications.

1.8.1. Differences between Artificial Intelligence (AI) and Natural Intelligence

Human intelligence, although it is amazing there is no exact definition, which means that none is sufficiently accurate and correct.

We can say that intelligence is the ability to deal with abstract symbols and relationships, to learn and to cope with new requirements, making proper use of thought or as a means for adapting new situations.

But questions about whether intelligence is inherited, acquired, influenced by the environment or a combination of these factors arise. Authors as fundamental as Luria or Piaget, intelligence interpreted as a quantitative variable that can be measured by a number (it is more or less intelligent as more or less high). For these authors, intelligence is the progressive development of a series of structures through different phases.

For other authors, intelligence increases from birth through experiences, reaching its peak in adolescence, posterior mind, at maturity, will notice a decline fairly slow, steady but not all intellectual abilities suffer the same deterioration.

There are other authors who give great importance to the heritage as Eysenck, this is a big proponent of the theory that intelligence is fundamentally unchangeable by education or the environment hereditary quality, this proved insufficient for the study of psychic phenomena for which controversy arose among geneticists.

We can say that if we believe in the superiority of heredity, we can do little. If you are born ready, this fact is as unchangeable as hair color or blood type. It is the environment that modulates and shapes intellectual capacity. We must affirm categorically that inheritance is necessary, but not sufficient to "make" a man. The mentality of the individual depends on structures, functions, norms, values and social models. Man is, in short, the result of two types of inheritance: biological and cultural.

Therefore, the human mind has no limits our potential is almost infinite, different texts and exhibitors raise the power of vision, dreams, the desire to do things, positive mental attitude.

We could say that the human being is endowed with skills to express ideas clearly, perspectives, thoughts, express feelings, to form mental models and maneuver, having a great capacity for abstract and mathematical reasoning ability with the body, understand, motivate, and help others, ability to realize and be able to differentiate between individuals their moods, intentions, motivations, temperament, emotions, experiences, to form a fair view of oneself and be able to use it to face life. These and many more are characteristic of the human being, and it clearly identified the difference in the biological brain and AI aspects.

Although the man has done everything possible to create a computer or robot able to perform similar to human tasks, this has not reached such a point that there is a learning, reasoning, perception, language, expressing emotions (laugh, mourn, angry, etc.), which are considered essential for intelligence.

So far it has built specialized machines for specific tasks, which at times are performed better than men, among them is the system Mycin applied to the field of medicine, which has obtained a percentage of successes in disease diagnosis higher than a physician infectious. Chess programs have beaten champions like Gary Kasparov; the computer that simulates the personality of a paranoid person; computers musicians who create musical compositions; and even a pianist who has played in the best orchestras in Japan. This shows that there is great similarity between computers and the human mind, but the difference is clear the mind of the human being goes beyond,

Unlike other operators, human intelligence is neural networks that interconnect the information stored partnership mechanisms triggering the activation of neural circuitry with specific functions to external and internal stimuli.

One can say that as time passes human intelligence develops improvements in the machines, trying to build a similar AI to human, without thinking more deeply about the different aspects of their individual and collective existence, or granting more importance to the understanding between man and man to man and machine that is produced.

The human desire to transcend the limitations to be deeply intertwined with the fascination of the technology, which can be as inspiring as frightening. How is being used it could profoundly change the character of our society, and irrevocably altering conceptions of ourselves, basically recognizing that as important as creating is not to destroy must move intelligently taking clear that builds to improve, becoming expert systems using it an effective tool in the service of man, but in a field of possibilities that exceed the conventional.

The most important difference between the brain and the computer is like it keeps your information. On your computer, your way of storing data is occupying a memory cell to store information, like when you want to access that information through the computer makes the call to that cell and displays the information. However, in the human brain, management is totally different, to access an array of information we do not make a call to that position the brain, do not even have a clear definition of how that information is stored and how does the brain to bring memory same information, we have no idea where X information is stored in our brain.

However, there is no need to have the exact location of the information and the fact only think or imagine some meaning and automatically the brain performs a function that human beings do not understand to bring our image this information, all this is done by the biological neural network. For example, consider wanting to imagine a square shape, the brain performs the action and we see in our mind this image of four side but at the same see, our brain is like Google, gives us other references in mental search engine and can see other similar forms squared and external figures, images that we remember seeing at some point and date given in our lives, even for example if we imagine a square piece of wood can access an array of the smell of the wood, the brain is a complex connection, all sense, all the connections are being used in one part of our brain to perform this simple task, is a profound mental game that we cannot explain so simply. The brain and the computer have their differences given as follows:

1. Brain:
- Data system capable of handling multi-purpose large amount of information in a short time but not necessarily accurately.
- The frequencies of nerve impulses can vary.
- It meets synapses in the brain called the simultaneous function of several gates.
- Memory is the associative and does not know where will be stored.
- The impulses flow 30 meters per second.

2. Computer:
- Highly specialized systems capable of processing very specific information, following instructions given.
- The transmission frequency is unchanged and is given by the internal clock of the machine.
- The logic gates have a perfectly determined and unalterable function.
- The information is stored in memory locations shortcuts for your address.
- Inside a computer impulses flow to the speed of light.

The similarities between the brain and the computer are as follows:
- Both encode information into digital pulses.
- Both the brain and the computer have logic gates.
- There are different types of memory.
- Both have about the same power consumption.

1.9. EXPERT SYSTEMS

An expert system is a computer system capable of emulating the ability of human decisions when faced with a particular type of problem. Expert systems are designed to solve complex problems by reasoning based on knowledge bases represented by rules "If, then" and not by regular procedures code. Expert systems are among the first successful attempts AI and start in the 70s and 80s.

Expert systems are divided into two subsystems which are the inference engine and knowledge base. The knowledge base represents realities and rules while the inference engine applies these rules to the facts to infer new facts.

Its applications are mostly in the area of business management and accounting, financial decisions, treasury, planning, and others. These functions involve the processing of large amounts of information and conducting complex in order to make decisions and that is why these expert systems are used mostly in these areas of mathematical operations.

More however not only at the enterprise level can be found these systems because it also applies in a number of areas such as military, computer, telecommunications, medicine, chemistry, electronics, transportation, etc.

Among its advantages, it is that expert systems are able to handle large amounts of information simultaneously and in turn, this is perhaps the greatest limitation of the human expert as this most likely will skip pieces of information that may think they are not as relevant directly affecting their decision making while the expert system will not miss any piece of information making a decision more solid and concise that it would take a human expert in a particular area.

Its disadvantages currently are that the system must be reprogrammed updated and are very flexible to change and difficult access to their information. Yet they have not been able to develop systems capable of solving problems generally or applying common sense to control ambiguous situations.

In the late 19th century, clarity about the work of the brain was achieved due to the work of Ramón and Cajal in Spain and Sherrington in England. The first work on the anatomy of neurons and second connection points thereof or synapses.

Nerve tissue is the most distinct of the organism and consists of nerve cells, nerve fibers, and neurology, which is formed by various kinds of cells. Nerve cells called neurons, the functional unit of the nervous system. There bipolar neurons, with two extensions of fibers and multipolar, with numerous extensions. They can be sensory, motor, and association neurons.

It is estimated that every millimeter of the brain there are about 50,000 neurons. The size and shape of neurons are variable, but the same subdivisions. The body or soma of the neuron containing core. It is responsible for all metabolic activities of the neuron and receives information from neighboring neurons through synaptic connections.

Dendrites are the input terminals of the neuron. Meanwhile, the axon is the "output" of the neuron and is used to send pulses or signals to other nerve cells. When the axon is close to its target cell divides into many branches that form synapses with the soma or axons from other cells. This union can be "inhibiting" or "exciter" that according to the transmitter release. Each neuron receives 10,000 to 100,000 synapses and the axon performs a similar amount of connections.

Transmitting a signal from one cell to another through the synapse is a chemical process. Transmitted substances are released into the transmitter side of the junction. The effect is to raise the electric potential or decrease within the body of the recipient cell. If your potential reaches the threshold, a pulse or action potential down the axon is sent. It is said, then, that the cell is fired. This pulse other neurons via axons distributions.

A biological neural network consists of input (sensors) connected to a complex network of neurons "calculators" (hidden neurons), which, in turn, are connected to neurons outputs that control, for example, muscle. Censors may be signs of the ears, eyes, etc. The responses of neurons Saluda activate the corresponding muscles. In the brain, there are gigantic res hidden neurons that perform the necessary computation. This similarly, an artificial neural network censor must be composed of mechanical or electrical.

As way how a biological neuron network, man has attempted to replicate this network of a technological form that can function much like human electrical impulses, including interconnection and final interface to execute the order by each neuron we can see an example like computer, a simple grid that takes the information, processes it and prints, all these elements are connected by buses or even every fiber on the motherboard so that everyone communicates with you or chip required to run what we need.

The artificial neuron is an electrical device that responds to electrical signals. Response reproduces the active circuit or transfers function part of the body of the neuron. The "dendrites" conduct electrical signals to the body of it. These signals come from sensors or are outputs of neighboring neurons. Signals on the dendrites may be positive or negative voltages; positive voltages contribute to the excitation of the body and negative voltages contribute to inhibit neuron response. All this is done by a mathematical calculation of binary language in which executes the process to perform the action.

1.9.1. Robotics

Robotics is a branch of technology that is dedicated to the design, construction, operation, and manufacturing robots.

Robotics is a combination of disciplines including mechanics have, electronics, computers, AI, engineering, and physics. Also in algebra are studied robotics, programmable logic controllers, animatronics, and state machines.

The term robot comes from the book RUR (robots universal Rossum) written by Karel Capek in 1920 in which the Czech word robot means forced or bonded labor is used.

Robotics is born of the human desire to create such machines itself able to lighten his work and for centuries begins with the construction of automatons were machines created with timepieces capable of performing certain tares but very limited way; its progress has not been as fast as in other areas of engineering but yet today we have much greater precision machines and easily programmable to perform specialized tasks such as in the automotive industry or the manufacture of high precision.

CHAPTER 2

General Concepts of Information Storage

CONTENTS

The information storage concept comes from the combination of two requirements that are not generally associated, however, they are taken together to get a better understanding of the problem and present a solution. These requirements are:

- Business requirement, from a broad perspective of company information.
- The need for information management by the IT department.

Taking them apart, demand for business requires a broad view of the information that may lead based allow any user to access any information no matter where it is located solutions. However, these solutions are simple, mainly because they ignore the distinction between data and information. In fact, what business users require is information (sometimes defined as data, in the business context).

Because of the way the applications are and as they continue to grow, they not only contain separate data business context but sometimes contain consistent data throughout the area of the company. Then the data are simply not suitable for direct use by end-users.

However combining the above needs, a new perspective is given. If the need for system management information data was taken into account, the need for extensive consultation business data business is easier to collect.

Similarly, the need for extensive consultation of the data and the obvious benefits of the business that they have, are the justification required to solve the problem of data management.

In the mid-1990s, the information storage began as a fad in the computer industry, has announced the value of the concept for more than a decade, you can see this development as a justification, such popularity brings its own problems. One of these is that initially, it leads sellers to adapt their particular concepts to make a connection between it and the goods they sell. It must be remembered that the information storage cannot be handled alone. This was invented by companies to meet their own needs, they continue to exist and continue to grow according to the technological environment in which businesses operate and become more complex.

Many of the key development computers are routed to the evolution of the information storage. The historical aspects are only general aspects, however, technical progress and business development are used as a yardstick against which measures the current situation in any company or part of it to understand how to best proceed.

Information storage is the center of the architecture for information systems (IS) in the nineties. It supports computer processing by providing a solid platform from historical data for analysis. It facilitates the integration of non-integrated application systems. It organizes and stores the data needed for analytical and computer processing on a broad perspective of time. Information storage is a collection of information-oriented topics, integrated, nonvolatile, time-variant, which is used to support the process of managerial decision making. It is characterized by a contrast of stored data from a business on it, unlike operational use by production applications. The entry into the information storage comes from the operational environment in almost all cases. This is an information storage transformed and physically separate from the application where the same in the operational environment.

2.1. INFORMATION SYSTEMS (IS)

IS have been divided according to the following scheme:

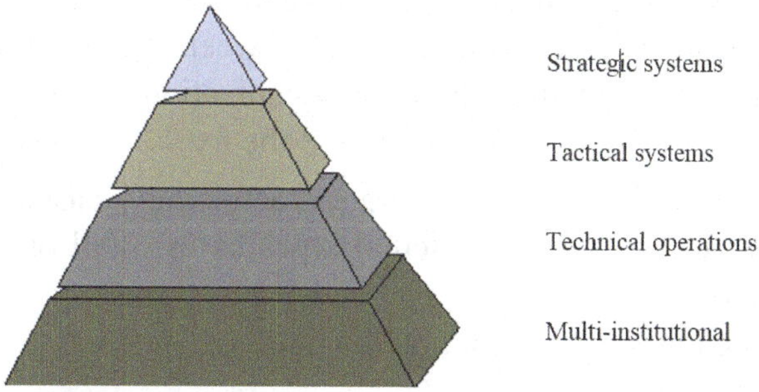

1. **Strategic Systems:** They are geared to support decision-making, facilitating the work of management, and providing basic support for decision-making. They are characterized because they are not periodic workload systems, namely, their use is not predictable. Prominent among them: The management information systems (MIS), executive information systems (EIS), geo-referential information systems (GIS), and systems business simulation (SBS).
2. **Tactical Systems:** Designed to support the coordination of activities and documentation management, defined to facilitate consultations on information stored in the system and

independent management of information by the intermediate levels of the organization. Highlights including: office systems (OA), transmission systems messaging (E-mail and fax server), coordination, and control tasks (workflow) systems and document processing (image processing and databases).

3. **Technical-Operating Systems:** These systems cover the core operations of mass traditional data capture and basic processing thereof with predefined tasks (accounting, billing, warehouse, budget, personnel, and other administrative systems). These are evolving with the introduction of sensors, automatons, multimedia, most advanced relational database, and information storage.
4. **Inter Systems:** This level of information systems is a consequence of organizational development aimed at a market of global nature, it forces us to think and implement structures closer communication between the organization and the market (extended enterprise, organization intelligence and integration organizational), all at from the generalization of computer networks national and global reach (INTERNET), which become a vehicle for communication between the organization and the market, no matter where the organization (intranet) is the market of the institution (extranet) and the market (global network).

However, the information storage technology based concepts and differences between two fundamental types of IS in all organizations: the technical and operational systems and decision support systems (DSS). The latter being the basis of information storage.

2.1.1. Technical and Operational Systems

They are those who help manage businesses in their daily operations. These operate on the backbone of any company or institution, including systems you have order entry, inventory, manufacturing, payroll, and accounting, among others.

Because of its size and importance in the organization, operational systems are always the first parts of the company to be computerized. Over the years, these operating systems have expanded, revised, improved, and maintained to the point that today are fully integrated into the organization. Of course, most of the largest of these worldwide, currently cannot operate without operational systems and data that these systems maintain.

2.1.2. Decision Support Systems (DSS)

There are functions within companies that have to do with planning, forecasting, and management of the organization. These functions are critical to the survival of organizations, especially in our rapidly changing world. Functions such as "marketing planning," "planning engineer," and "financial analysis" require IS that support. But these functions are different from operational and types of required systems. The knowledge-based functions are DSS.

These systems are related to data analysis and decision-making, often, they are important to know how the company operates, now, and in the future. These not only have a different approach to operational, but have a different scope. While the needs of operational data are usually geared to a single area, data to support decisions often take a number of different areas and require large amounts of related operational data. Are these systems on which the information storage technology is based?

Both methods have evolved over time and now organizations manage not clean and inconsistent data, on which, most often, important decisions are made. Administrative management recognizes that one way to increase efficiency is to make the best use of information resources that already exist within the organization. However, even though this has been trying for many years, there is no effective use of them.

The main reason is the way computers have evolved based on information technologies and systems. Most organizations do their best to get good information, but achieving that goal depends primarily on its current architecture, both hardware and software.

The information storage is currently the focus of large institutions, because it provides an environment for organizations to make better use of the information is managed by various operational applications. Information storage is a collection of data in which information is integrated Institution and used as support for the process of making management decisions. Although various organizations and individuals fail to understand the approach of a warehouse, experience has shown that there are many potential pitfalls.

Gather the appropriate data elements from various sources into a centralized integrated application environment, simplifies the problem of access to information and thus speeds up the process of analysis, consultation, and shorter use of information. Applications for decision support based on an information storage, can make more practical and easy exploitation of data for greater business efficiency, which is not achieved when using only the data from operational applications (which help in operation of the company in its daily operations), in which information is obtained by separate processes and often complex.

Information storage is created by extracting data from one or more databases of operational applications. The extracted data is processed to remove inconsistencies and summarize if necessary and then loaded into the information storage. The process of transforming, creating detail variant time sum and combine the extracts data, help create the environment for access to corporate information. This new approach helps individuals, at all levels of the company, to make their decisions more responsibly.

The innovation of information technology within an environment information storage can allow any organization to make optimal use of data as a key ingredient for making process more effective decisions. Organizations need to leverage their information resources to create the information business operation, but should be considered technological strategies needed to implement a complete information storage architecture.

2.2. DEFINITION OF INFORMATION STORAGE

In competitive business environments today, understand and manage information is crucial for companies to make timely decisions responding to business changes. Applications processing data has proliferated across a wide variety of operating systems over the past two decades, complicating the task of locating and integrating data for decision support, taking an authoritative decision distribution starts at all levels of the organization. More people need access to the information necessary for making a business decision. As a result of this competitively handle and use, many organizations are now building information storage.

Information storage supports business analysis and decisions made for the creation of an integrated database, consistently oriented themes, and historical information. It integrates data from multiple heterogeneous systems to a consolidated database. In the transformation of these, it allows business managers to make a more substantive consistent and accurate analysis. Significant cost benefits, time, and productivity are associated with the use of information storage in processing information. First, the data are easily accessed and analyzed without consuming time, handling, and processing. Decisions are made faster and the confidentiality of the data is accurate. Integrated information is maintained in categories that are meaningful to produce an operation. The trends are analyzed and predicted with available historical data. Information storage ensures that all the same data extracted at the same level, eliminating conflicting test results and arguments that do not match the source and quality of data used in the analysis. In short, it enables information to be processed in an efficient and credible. Information storage has the following aspects:

- All the information is collected in a company and is placed in a management system database.
- It is a set of information integration tools designed for the purpose of facilitating decision-making.
- It is a solution that allows you to examine historical data and analyze it in different ways making decisions based on them.

2.2.1. Oriented Topics

A first feature of the information storage is that information on aspects that are of interest to the company is classified based. Data being taken in contrast to the classical process-oriented applications.

Figure 2.1 shows the contrast between the two types of orientations.

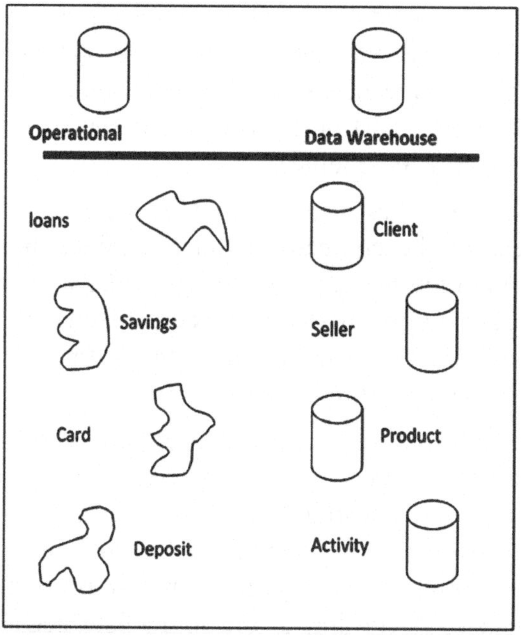

Figure 2.1. The contrast between the two types of orientations.

The operational environment is designed around applications and functions such as loans, savings, credit cards, and deposits to a financial institution. For example, an order entry application can access data about customers, products, and accounts. The database combines these elements in a structure that accommodates the needs of the application.

The information storage environment is organized around subjects such as customers, vendors, products, and activities. For example, for a manufacturer, these are customers, products, suppliers, and vendors. For a university can be students, classes, and teachers. For a hospital can be patient, medical personnel, medicines.

Applications are related to the design of the database and process. The information storage focuses on data modeling and the design of the database. Differences between the orientation process and application functions and guidance issues lie in the content of the data at a detailed level. In the information storage information is not used by the process systems decision support, it is excluded while the information-oriented applications, contain data immediately meet the functional requirements and process that can be used or not the decision support analyst.

Another important difference is in the interrelation of information. Operational data maintained an ongoing relationship between two or more tables based on a business rule that is in effect. The rules of the information storage measure time and relationships found each other. Many of trade rules (and corresponding data relationships) are represented in the information storage, between two or more tables.

In short, oriented topics means that it is organized in relation to the core subject areas of the company. Guidance about the most important issues of the corporation because the design of the information storage is handling data. Data handling matters of this organization is in contrast to the classical/functional process of the applications of the organization, which characterizes the older operating systems.

The world of information storage is organized in relation to the most important subjects of the areas of the corporation, which affect the design and implementation in the search data to the information storage. Another important distinction between oriented applications and operational data contained in the information storage is the relationship these. Operational applications are listed according to the immediate needs concerning the business, which is accurate and relevant right now. A relationship in the operational environment is based on the current rules of the business relationship going on between two or more tables or databases.

2.2.2. Integrated Topics

The most important aspect of the information storage environment is that the information found within it is integrated. This data integration is shown in many ways: in consistent naming conventions in the uniform measure variables in coding structures, physical attributes of the data, multiple sources, and others. The contrast of integration found in the information storage with the lack of integration applications environment, with their respective differences are shown in Figure 2.1

Over the years, designers of different applications make their own decisions about how it should build an application. Styles and custom designs are shown in various ways. They differ in coding in the key structures in their physical characteristics, naming conventions, and others. Figure 2.1 shows some of the major differences in the ways in which applications are designed.

- **Coding:** Application designers encode the GENERO field in several ways. These represent GENERO as "M" and "F" others as a "1" and "0," others as "X" and "Y" and even as "male" and "female." No matter how gender arrives at the information storage, probably "M" and "F" are as good as any other representation. The important thing is that gender should reach the information storage integrated in a state uniform. Therefore, when gender is loaded into the information storage from an application, which has been represented in the format "M" and "F," data must be converted to the format of the information storage that not exactly be the same.
- **As Attribute:** Application designers obtained measurement units in a variety of ways. A designer stores data in centimeters, inches others, others in million cubic feet per second and others in yards. By taking measures to attributes, the processing translates the various units used in the different databases to transform them into a common standard. Whatever the source, when the information reaches the information storage needs to be measured in the same way.

- **Naming Conventions:** The same element is often referred to by different names in different applications. The transformation process ensures that the user name is preferably used.
- **Multiple Sources:** The same element can be derived from multiple sources. In this case, the transformation process must ensure that the proper source is used, documented, and moved to the tank (Figure 2.2).

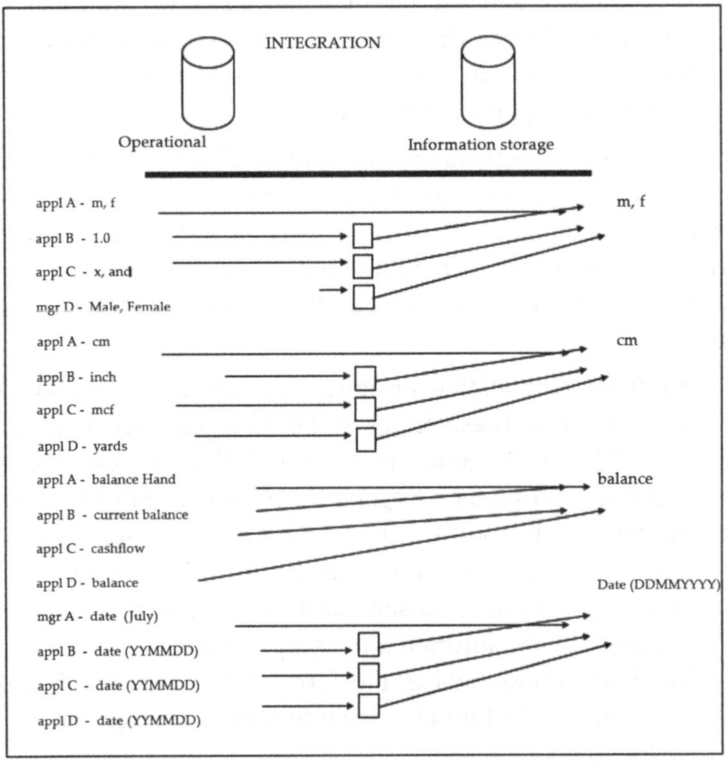

Figure 2.1. The integration points.

As shown in the figure, the integration points affect almost every aspect of the design (the physical characteristics of the data, the incompatibility of having more than one data source, the problem of standards inconsistent naming, formats inconsistent date, whatever the shape of the design, the result is the same) information needs to be stored in the information storage in a globally acceptable and unique model, even though the operating systems store data differently.

When the analyst DSS observes the information storage, your focus should be on the use of the data that is in the tank, before wondering about the reliability or consistency of the data.

This is the most important feature of information storage. With this application, it takes a very corporate taste. The integration of the data shows many different routes consistent naming conventions, measures of variables, coding structures, physical attributes of data, among others. Contrast the information found with the lack of integration in application environments. As the years passed, many designers have made their individual decisions on how an application should be built. The style and design decisions tailored by the designer show many ways, as well as differences in coding, differences in key structures, physical characteristics, including naming conventions.

As editing design, the result is the same: the data need to be stored in the information storage uniquely, globally accepted even when the main operational systems store data differently.

2.2.3. Time Variant Systems

All information from the information storage is required at some point. This basic characteristic of the data in a reservoir is very different from the information found in the operational environment. In these, the information is required at the time of access. In other words, in the operational environment, it accesses an information unit that is expected that the required values are obtained from the time of access.

As information in the information storage is requested at any time (i.e., not "right now"), the data found in the reservoir are called "variant time." Historical data are of little use in operational processing. Deposit information should include historical data for use in identifying and assessing trends (see Figure 2.3).

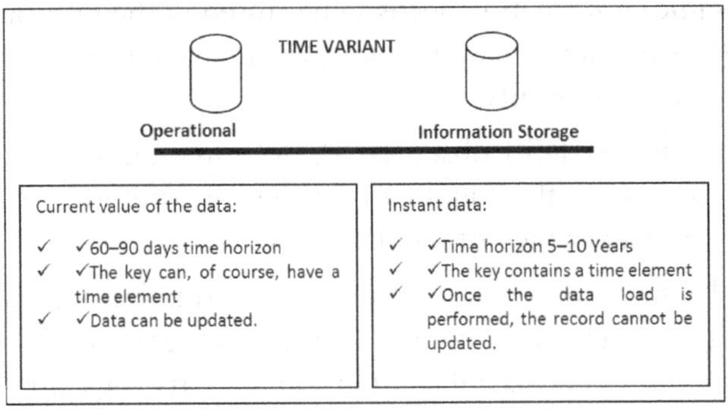

Figure 2.2. Identifying and assessing trends.

The time-variant shown in several ways:

- The simplest is that information represents data over a long time horizon (from five to ten years). The time horizon represented for the operational environment is much shorter from current values up to sixty to ninety days.

  Applications that perform well and are available for processing transactions must carry a minimum amount of data and some degree of flexibility. Therefore, operational applications have a short time horizon, due to the design of rigid applications.

- The second way is showing the time variation in the information storage is the key structure. Each key structure contains, implicitly or explicitly, a time element as day, week, and month.

  The time element is almost always the key in the information storage. Sometimes, the time element exists implicitly, as the case where an entire file is doubled at the end of the month or the quarter.

- The third way the time is displayed variant is when the information storage, once properly registered, cannot be updated. The information contained in this is, for all practical purposes, a long series of snapshots views (snapshots).

If the view snapshots of the data are taken incorrectly, they can be changed. Assuming that the snapshot views have been properly taken, they are not altered once made. In some cases is unethical, alter the view snapshots in the information storage. Operational data are required from the time of access and can be updated as needed.

All data in the information storage is accurate at any moment in time. This basic feature is very different from the data found in the operational environment. In this environment, the data is accurate at the time of access. In other words, in an operational environment, when they are accessed, it is expected to reflect accurate values at the time of access.

The variance in the time data information storage sample in several ways. Running applications are available for transaction processing; they must carry the same amount of data if they have some degree of flexibility. Therefore, operational applications have a short time horizon. The structure is a way in which the variance of time shown in the information storage.

2.2.4. Nonvolatile Systems

Information is useful only when it is stable. Operational data change on a moment-to-moment basis. Essential for analysis and decision-making perspective, requires a stable database.

Figure 2.3 shows that the update (add, delete, and modify) is done regularly in the operational environment on a record basis. But the basic data manipulation occurring in the information storage is much simpler. There are only two types of operations: the initial loading of data and access to them. No update in the tank, as a normal part of the process.

There are some very important consequences of this basic difference between operational processing and information storage. At the design level, they need to be cautious to update anomalies is not a factor in this, since the data update is not done. This means that in the physical level of design freedom can be taken to improve access to data, particularly when using standardization and physical normalization.

Another consequence of the simplicity of operation of the information storage is in the technology used to run the data in the warehouse. Having to support, the update of each record in online mode (as is common in the case of operational processing) requires that technology has a very complex foundation beneath a facade of simplicity (Figure 2.4).

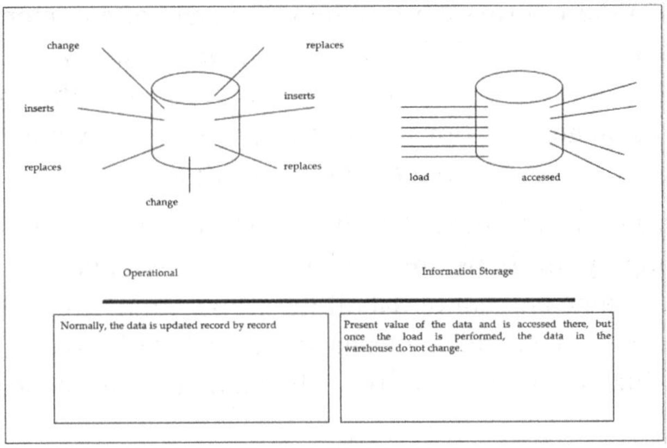

Figure 2.3. The data loaded into the information storage.

In information storage, the processing is not necessary. The source of most information is the operational environment. At first glance, you may think there is massive redundancy of data between the two environments. The first impression of many people focuses on large data redundancy between the operational environment and atmosphere of information storage. Such reasoning is superficial and demonstrates a lack of understanding regarding what happens in the information storage. In fact, there is minimal data redundancy between the two environments.

You should consider the following:

- The data is filtered when they pass through the reservoir's operational environment. There are data that never leave the operational environment. Only the data needed to enter the information storage environment.
- The time horizon of data is different from one environment to another. The information in the operational environment is new with respect to information storage. From the perspective of the unique time horizons, there is little overlap between the operational environments and information storage.
- The information storage contains a summary of information not found in the operational environment.
- Data undergo a fundamental transformation when passing information storage. Most significantly alter the data to be selected and moved toward him. In other words, most of the data is altered physical and radically when they move to the tank. There are the same data residing in the operational environment from the standpoint of integration.

In view of these factors, data redundancy between the two environments is a rare occurrence, resulting in less than 1%.

In short, updates, insertions, deletions, and changes are made regularly in the operational environment. But the basic data manipulation occurring in the information storage is very simple. There are two kinds of operations occurring in it, loading, and data access only. No update at this as a normal part of the process. There are powerful consequences of these basic differences between the operational processing and processing of information storage. In design, the need to be wary of update anomalies is not a factor in this, because an update is not done. This means that the scope of physical design can take some liberties to optimize data access, particularly in dealing with the benefits of standardization and physical normalization.

2.3. THE STRUCTURE OF INFORMATION STORAGE

There are different structures for information storage. There are different levels of outlining and detail that define. The different components are shown and are:

- **Details of Current Data:** The most important interest lies in the detail of the current data, because:
  - or Reflect the most recent occurrences, which are of great interest.
  - or It is bulky as it is stored at the lowest level of granularity.
  - or Always stored on disk, it is easily accessible, although its administration is costly and complex.
- **Details of Old Data:** Details that are stored on some form of mass storage. They are not frequently accessed and stored at a level of detail consisting of current detailed data. While priority is not stored in a storage medium alternative, because of the large volume of data and no frequent access to them, it is unusual to use the disk as a storage medium.
- **Summarized Data:** Data that come from a low level of detail found the current level of detail. This is always stored on disk (Figure 2.5). The points where the designer is based to build are:
  - The unit time is over flowcharting made.
  - Content (attributes) have slightly summary data.
- **Fully Summarized Data:** These data are compact and easily accessible.

- **Metadata:** The final component of the information storage is the metadata. In many ways, this is in a different data than other information storage dimension, because its content is not taken directly from the operational environment.

The metadata plays a special and very important role in the information storage and is used as:

- a directory to help the analyst to locate the contents of the information storage;
- a guide for mapping data processing, operational to the information storage environment; or
- a guide to the algorithms used for schematization between current data detail with slightly summarized and these, with fully summary data.

Metadata plays an important role in that classic information storage operational environment. To remember the different levels of data found in the information storage, it considers the example shown in Figure 2.6.

The detail of old sales is found before 1998. However, the full details of sales since 1988 (or when the designer began the collection of files) are stored in the level of detail oldest data.

The current detail contains information from 1998 to 1999. Overall, sales are located at the current level until you pass at least twenty-four hours until the sales information is available in the operational environment.

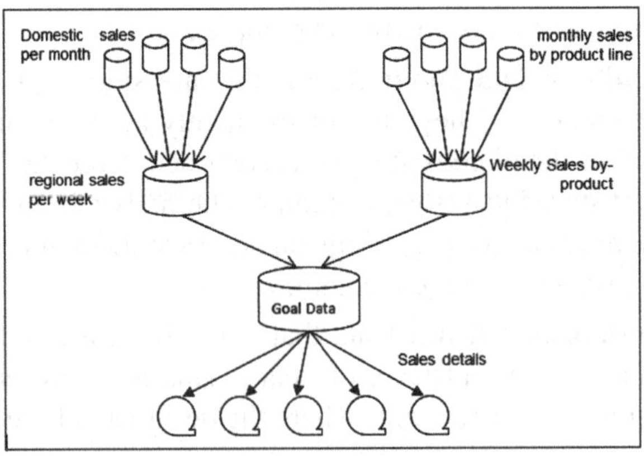

Figure 2.4. Different levels of data found in the information storage.

There is a 24-hour delay between the time when the operating environment a new sales income is made and when the sale information has entered the information storage. The breakdown of sales is summarized weekly by product line and region to produce slightly smaller data storage. The breakdown of sales is added weekly monthly, according to a range of lines to produce fully consolidated data.

Generally, the metadata contains:

- The data structure;
- The algorithms used for flowcharting;
- The mapping from the operational environment to information storage.

Additional information that is not diagrammed is stored in the information storage. Sometimes the analysis is done and a type of synbook occurs. The only type of program that is permanently stored in the information storage is the data that are frequently used. If an analyst produces a scheme that has a very low probability of being used again, then it is not stored in the information storage.

2.4. ARCHITECTURE OF INFORMATION STORAGE

The reason why the development of information storage grows rapidly, it is because it really is a very understandable technology. In fact, it represents the broad structure of a company to manage the informational data within the organization. To understand how all the components involved in a strategy related to information storage is essential to have an architecture for this.

Information storage architecture (ISA) is the way to represent the entire data structure, such as communication, processing, and presentation, this exists for end-users who have a computer within the company.

The architecture is made up of interconnected parts:

- **Base Operational/Level External Database Data:** Operating systems process data to support critical operations needs. To do that, we have created the basis of historical operational data that provides an efficient processing structure for a relatively small number of well-defined business transactions. However, because of the narrow focus of operational systems, databases designed to support these, have difficulty accessing data for other purposes or computer management. This is amplified by the fact that many of these systems are 10 to 15 years old. Time some of these systems means that the access technology available data for operational data is old.

The goal of the information storage is to release the information stored in operational databases and combine it with information from another data source, usually external. Increasingly, large organizations acquire additional data from external databases.

- **Level of Access to Information:** It is the level that the end-user is directly responsible. In particular, it represents the tools that this normally uses daily. This level includes hardware and software that display information on screen printing and issuing reports, spreadsheets, graphs, and charts for analysis and presentation. Two decades ago, the level of access to information has expanded enormously, especially for end-users who have turned to the single PCs and networked PCs.

Currently, there are sophisticated techniques for manipulating, analyzing, and presenting data; however, there are significant problems when trying to convert the data as it is collected and which are contained in the operational systems easy and transparent information tools user's finals. One of the keys to this is to find a common language of data that is used throughout the company.

- **Level Data Access:** The level of access to data from the information storage architecture engages with the level of access to information to discuss at the operational level. In today's global network, common data language arises SQL (structured query language). Originally, SQL was developed by IBM as a query language, but in the last twenty years has become the standard for data exchange.

The level of access to data not only connects DBMSs (relational databases) and different file systems on the same hardware, but also manufacturers and network protocols. One of the keys to an information storage strategy is to provide end-users with "universal access to data." Access to universal data means that, theoretically at least, the final regardless of tool access to information or location users should be able to access any or all data in the enterprise which is necessary for them. The level of access to data then is responsible for the interface between the tools of access to information and operational databases. In some cases, this is everything an end-user needs.

- **Level Data Directory (Metadata):** In order to provide universal access to data, it is absolutely necessary to maintain some form of directory data or metadata repository information. In order to have a fully functional deposit, you need to have a variety of metadata available, information about the views of end-user data and information on operational databases. Ideally, end users should access data from the information storage (or from the operational databases), without having to know where the data resides or how they are stored.

- **Process Management Level:** The level of process management has to do with scheduling various tasks to be done to build and maintain the information storage and data directory information. This level may depend on the high level of job control for many processes that must occur to keep the information storage updated.
- **Message Level Application:** The level of application message has to do with transporting information around the enterprise network. The application message also referred to as "product," but may involve only network protocols. It can be used for example to isolate operational or strategic applications from exact data format, collect transactions or messages and deliver them to a safe location at a certain time.
- **Level Information Storage (Physical):** In the information storage it is where the current data, mainly used for strategic uses occur. In some cases, you can think of information storage simply as a logical or virtual data view. In many instances, information storage may not involve data storage. In information storage physical copies, in some cases, many copies of operational and/or external data are actually stored in a way that is easy to access and is highly flexible. Increasingly, the information storage is stored on client/server platforms, but usually stored on mainframes or large computers.
- **Organization Level Data:** The final component of the information storage architecture is the organization of data. Copy or replica management is also called, but in fact, it includes all necessary processes such as select, edit, summarizes, combine, and load data into the repository and access information from operational databases and/or external.

2.5. OPERATIONS IN INFORMATION STORAGE

1. **Operating Systems:** The data managed by operational application

systems are the main source of data for information storage. The operational databases are organized as indexed files, databases, network/systems hierarchical or relational database.

2. Extraction, Transformation, and Loading Data: Data management tools are required to extract data from databases and/or operational files, and then you need to manipulate or transform data before loading the results in the information storage. Take data from several operational databases and transforming it into data required for the deposit, it refers to the transformation or integration of data. The operational databases designed to support various production applications often differ in format. The same data elements, if used by different or administered by different software administration database (DBMS) applications, may be defined by using names inconsistent elements that have inconsistent and/or be encoded differently formats.

3. **Metadata:** Another necessary step is to create the metadata. This describes the contents of the information storage. It consists of definitions of data elements in the tank, systems source elements. Data, integrate, and transform before being stored in similar information.

4. **End-User Access:** These they access the information storage using productivity tools based graphical user interface (GUI). Provide users of the information storage many of these types of instruments. These may include query software, report generators, online analytical processing (OLAP), data/visual mining, etc., depending on the types of users and their particular requirements. However, one does not satisfy everyone, so that the integration of a number of utilities is necessary.

5. **Information Storage Platform:** The platform for information storage is almost always a server relational database. When very large volumes of data handled may be required configuration block. Extracts of integrated/transformed data are loaded into the information storage. The choice of platform is critical. The deposit grows and you need to understand the requirements after 3 or 5 years. Many organizations want or do not choose a platform for various reasons: the X system is chosen or Y is available on the one you already have. One of the biggest mistakes organizations make when selecting the platform is that they assume that the

(hardware and/or DBMS) system scale data.

The deposit system executes the queries passed to the data access software user. Although one of these displays queries from the point of view of a GUI, these are typically formulated as SQL requests, because it is a universal language and the fact standard for data access.

6. **External Data:** Depending on the application, the scope of the information storage extends the ability to access external data. For example, the data accessible via online computer services and/or via the internet may be available to users of the information storage.
7. **Evolution of Deposit:** Building information storage is a big task. It is not advisable to undertake development in the company as a project either. Rather, it is recommended that the requirements of a number of phases are developed and implemented in consecutive models that allow the more gradual process and iterative completion. There is no organization to succeed in the development of information storage company, in one step. Many have achieved after a development step. Previous advances evolve together with the material being added.

Data in the information storage are non-volatile and is a read-only repository. However, new elements can be added on a regular basis for the content follow the evolution of these in the source database, both in terms of content and time. One of the challenges of maintaining information storage is to devise methods to identify new or modified in operational database information. Some ways to identify include insert date/time records and then create and copy updated copies of transaction records and/or based on daily data. These new and/or modified elements are extracted, integrated, processed, and added to the information storage in newspapers programmed steps. As new occurrences are added, the old data is deleted.

2.6. DATA TRANSFORMATION AND METADATA

The challenge of any implementation of information storage is to transform the data. These handle inconsistencies in the formats and coding that can exist within a single database and that there are almost always when multiple databases contribute constitute it. Figure 2.5 illustrates an inconsistency, wherein the genus is coded differently in three databases. Transformation processes are developed to route them inconsistencies (Figure 2.5).

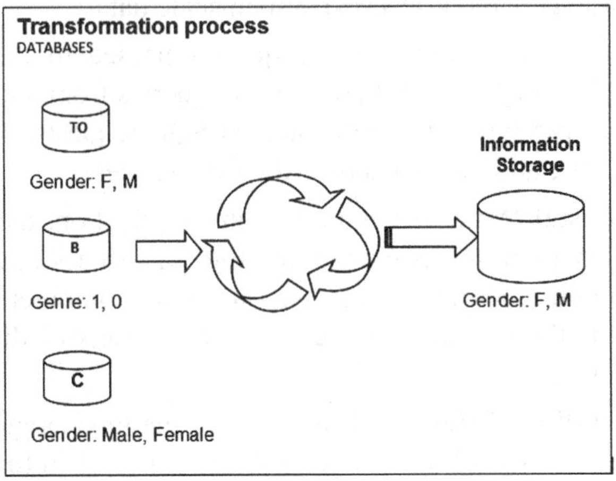

Figure 2.5. Transformation processes.

Data transformation is also responsible for inconsistencies in the content of these. Once the decision on the transformation rules needed is taken, you create and include definitions modification routines. Careful and detailed planning is required to transform reconcilable inconsistent and consistent data to load into the information storage sets.

Another aspect of the architecture is to create information storage supports the metadata. It is a generic concept, but each implementation of these specific methods and techniques used. These are dependent on the requirements of each organization, existing capabilities, and user interface requirements. There are no standards for metadata, so it must be defined from the point of view of software for information storage selected.

The metadata includes the following aspects:

- Data structures that give an insight to the administrator.
- The definitions of the registration system from which the information storage is built.
- Specifications data transformations that occur as the source is replicated to the information storage.
- The data model information storage (i.e., the elements and their relationships).
- A record of when new items are added to the information storage and when old are removed or summarized.

- Levels and method of summarization tables and records of your information storage.

Some implementations of metadata definitions include the views presented to users of the information storage. They are defined to favor the varied preferences of different user groups. In implementations, these descriptions are stored in an information catalog. Subschem as schemes and operational databases to form the optimal input source when the metadata is created. Make use of existing documentation, especially when it is available electronically, accelerates the process of defining the metadata. This serves in a sense as the heart of an information storage environment. Create a complete and effective definition is a time-consuming process, but most of the definitions are efforts resulting in the maintenance of information storage.

2.7. DATA FLOW

There is a normal and predictable flow of data within the information storage. Figure 2.6shows that flow. Information enters the information storage from the operational environment. When introduced to the information storage, go to the current level of detail. It stays there and is used until one of the following three events (Figure 2.6):

- It is removed;
- It summarizes; and
- It is archived.

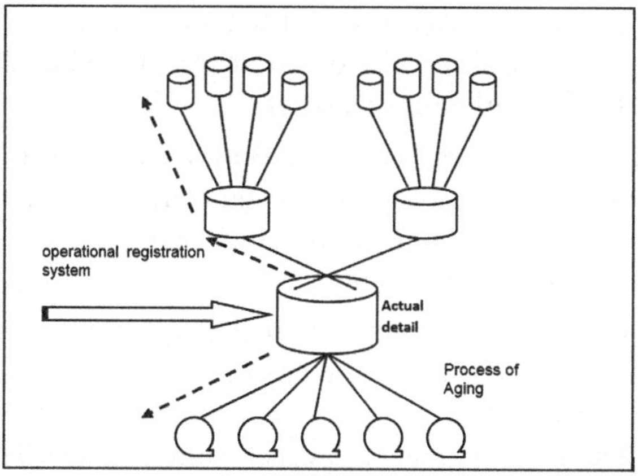

Figure 2.6. Datastream of information storage.

With the process of downgrading information storage detail of old current data, based on the timing of these moves. The process schematization used to calculate detail in light and fully condensed form.

2.8. INFORMATION STORAGE USES

Operational data and information storage are accessed by users who use them in different ways. the differences are shown in the following table:

Use of Operational Database	Use of Information Storage
Many concurrent users.	Few concurrent users.
Predefined queries and updated.	Complex queries, often unanticipated.
Small amounts of detailed data.	Large amounts of detailed data.
Immediate response requirements.	Noncritical response requirements.

Users need to access an information storage complex data, often from multiple sources and unpredictable ways. When they access operational, they perform predefined, generally require access to database application tasks. On the contrary, those who access information storage, perform tasks that require access to a set of data from multiple sources and are not predictable. All that is known is the initial set of data that has been established in the tank. For example, a specialist in health care needs access to current and historical cost analyzes trends using a set of predefined queries. By contrast, a sales representative needs access to customer and product data to evaluate the effectiveness of a marketing campaign.

- **Only a Few Users Access the Data Concurrently:** In contrast to the production of systems that can handle hundreds or thousands of concurrent users, the information storage accesses a limited set of users at any given time.
- **Users Generate Unpredictable Complex Processing:** Complex queries are generated. The answer to a query formulation leads to more detailed questions, in a process starting at the highest level and down to detail levels (drilling down). The information storage can include multiple summaries, derived from a core set, unique, detailed data to support such use.

Users often start looking at the data summarized as identify areas of interest; they begin to access the detailed set. The summary sets represent the "why" of a situation and detailed sets allow users to build a picture of "How" is derived from that situation.

- **Queries Access Large Amounts of Data:** Because of the need to investigate trends and evaluate relationships between many kinds of data, the information storage queries allow access to very large volumes both detailed and summary. Due to the requirements of historical data, the information storage evolves to reach a larger size than its operational origins (10 to 100 times larger).
- **Queries Do Not Have Critical Response Times:** Operational transactions require an immediate response because a customer may be expecting a solution. In the information storage, on the other hand, it has a requirement for non-critical response because the result often is used in a process of analysis and decision-making. Although response times are not critical, users expect a resolution within the same day it is made the query.

Generally, levels of data within the information storage are different uses. A higher level of flowcharting, have increased use of these. There is good reason to move an organization paradigm suggested in Figure 2.6 the use of the resource. The data summarized, allow capture them quickly and efficiently. If a processing task much detail levels information storage is done, then many machine resources consumed. It is better to do the processing at higher levels of flowcharting.

For many tasks, the systems analyst uses decision-support information at the level of detail in a predating warehouse. The security detail is achieved in many ways, even though other flowcharting levels are available. An activity designer is to disconnect the system user decision support constant use of data at the lowest detail.

The designer has two predispositions data:

- Installing a system where the end-user pays for the resources consumed; and
- Report the best response time obtainable when working with data at a high level of schematization, unlike a poor response time resulting from working with low details.

2.9. ADVANTAGES AND DISADVANTAGES OF INFORMATION STORAGE

Build information storage can give companies strategic advantages over the competition. These advantages come from several sources:

- **Access to All Company Information:** information from different source systems are consolidated, regardless of whether they come from the same source or sources.
- **Consistency of Information:** It is achieved by various departments to make the information consistent. It is easier for decision making with consolidated information separate.
- **Ease of Data Analysis:** Having the information already stored and consolidated easier the analysis of it.
- **Integration of Data from Multiple Incompatible Systems to a Consolidated Database:** Conduct an information storage that provides the advantage of obtaining information from multiple sources of information regardless of compatibility between the two. This is done via ODBC or OLEDB.
- **Cost Benefits, time, and Productivity:** AI information storage helps you get better response times and improves the production process.

It is said that if a company wants good business, make better decisions close to customers and competitive advantage, ideally implement an information storage to help you get these benefits.

2.10. EXAMPLE OF INFORMATION STORAGE

To illustrate how an information storage can help an organization improve its operations, an example of which is the development of activities without an information storage shown.

The preparation of a report is considered a fairly typical problem in a large manufacturing company in which information (a report) that is not available is requested. The current report includes financial, inventory, and personnel status, together with comparisons with the previous current month and the same month last year, with a further comparison of the three preceding years. Should explain every deviation from the trend that falls outside a predefined range. Without an information storage, the report is prepared as follows:

The financial information obtained from a database through a program of data mining, the inventory of another program from another database, the status of staff of a third extraction program and historical information from a backup tape or CD ROM.

The most interesting is that another report continues the first report (because the questions originated from the above) calls. The fact is that none of the work done so far (for example, various extraction programs) is used for the next or any subsequent report. Time and effort has been wasted by an outdated approach are very big. This example is shown in Figure 2.7 The inconsistencies are identified in each set of extracted data and resolved, usually manually. When all this processing is completed, the report is formatted, printed, reviewed, and transmitted. Again, the important point here is that all work performed for this report does not affect other reports that may be requested (Figure 2.9).

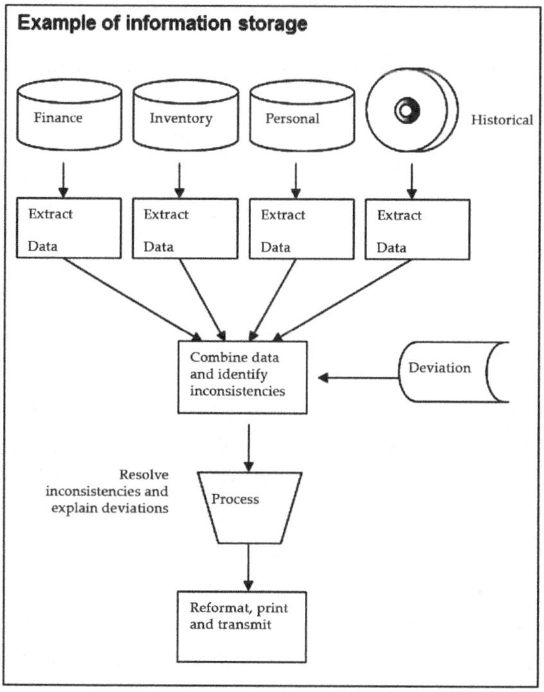

Figure 2.7. Example of information storage.

When creating information storage and combine all the required data, the following benefits:

- Data inconsistencies are resolved automatically when items are loaded into the information storage, each time a report is prepared.
- Errors that occur during the complex process of preparing the report are minimized because the process is now simpler.
- The data are easily accessible for other uses, not only for a particular report.
- One source is created.

2.11. ADDITIONAL CONSIDERATIONS

There are additional considerations that are taken into account when constructing and managing the information storage:

- Index: Information at higher levels can be freely indexed, while low levels of detail, for being so bulky, can be indexed moderately. Therefore, the data at high detail levels are easily restructured, while the volume of data in the lower levels is so great that the data is not easily restructured. Therefore, the data model and classic design underlying the information storage are applied only to the current level of detail. In other words, the data modeling activities do not apply to schemed levels, in almost all cases.
- Partition Information in the Information Storage: The current level of detail is always partitioned. The partition is done in two ways: the level of DBMS and application level. In the DBMS partition, partitions are known and managed accordingly. In the case of the partition of applications, only programmers know them partitions and management responsibility is assigned to them. Inside the DBMS partitions, many of the infrastructure works are done automatically. But there is a high degree of stiffness associated with automatic management of partitions. For partitions information storage applications, most of the work falls on the programmer, but the end result is that data management is more flexible.

2.12. EXCEPTIONS IN THE INFORMATION STORAGE

While information storage components work according to the model described for almost all data, there are few useful exceptions discussed:

- **Public Summary Data:** Are the data outside the information storage calculated but are used by the corporation. Public summary data are stored and managed in the information storage, although its calculation has been made out of it.
- **External Data:** They are considered as an exception.
- **Detail of Permanent Data:** Results from the need to store corporate data at a detailed level permanently for ethical or legal reasons. If corporation workers exposed to hazardous substances there is a need for permanent data detail. If a product in a corporation involving public safety occurs, such as the construction of aircraft parts, there is a permanent need. If a corporation commits to dangerous contracts, there is a need for permanent data detail.

Organizations do not leave the details because in future years, in the event of a lawsuit, a notification, a building in dispute, etc., exposing the company increases. Therefore, there is only one type of data in the information storage known as "permanent detail data." It shares the same considerations as another information storage, except that:

- The medium where the data is stored must be safe.
- The data should allow to be restored.

Data need special treatment in indexing, as otherwise may not be accessible even if it is stored with security.

CHAPTER 3

Production Process for Information Storage

CONTENTS

3.1. ORGANIZATION

Planning is the most important process that determines the type of strategies that an organization's information storage starts. For this reason, the following points are taken into account.

3.1.1. Information Gathering

- **Understanding the Business Process:** Primarily, it needs to be clear as the administrative business cycle works, understand the mission, vision, and objectives of it, since this depends on the good or bad design information storage.
- **Identifying Objects, Events, and Key Indicators:** Within the management process are key processes that are what really defines the business running. Each of these is identified in order to know what are the influencing factors in this cycle are. Events like these are all actions or events in time that are important in the flow of information that takes place in the company, and therefore identifying the above objects and events, key indicators are obtained.
- **Identify Dimensions, Data, and Hierarchies:** Based on the requirements necessary weapon with which an information storage, this step is an indispensable part of the process. The dimensions help define the sides of the detail information, taking clear beforehand that they follow the hierarchy. In every company, there are data that are more significant than others, and that at any given time are essential for decision-making. Good identification of these is reflected in the presentation of the data.

These three points cover the process of gathering information. After this analysis is feasible to start creating information storage.

3.1.2. Factors in Planning a Storage Information

There is no security formula for successful building an information storage, but there are many points that contribute to that goal. Here are some key points considered in planning an information storage indicated:

1. **Establish an Association of Users and Groups Management:** Both users and management who ensure that the information storage contains information that meets the requirements of the company involved. Management helps to prioritize the

implementation phase of the information storage, as well as the selection of user tools. These justify the costs of information storage on how "the environment" and is based first on what is expected and second, in the real commercial value.

2. **Select a Pilot Application with a High Probability of Success:** A pilot application limited in scope, with a measurable reimbursement for users and management sets the information storage as a key technology for the company. These same criteria (limited scope, measurable reimbursement, and clear benefits for the company) are applied to each phase of the implementation of an information storage.
3. **Build Prototypes quickly and frequently:** The only way to ensure that the information storage meets the needs of users is to make the prototype throughout the implementation process and beyond, so the new data and/or models permanently added. Continued work with users and management is the key.
4. **Incremental Implementation:** Incremental deployment reduces risk and ensures that the size manageable permanent project at every stage.
5. **Actively Report and Publish Success Stories:** User feedback provides an excellent opportunity to publish the facts successful within an organization. Internal publicity about how the information storage has helped users to operate effectively supports construction throughout an enterprise.

User feedback helps us to understand the evolving implementation of information storage over time to gather user requirements identified again.

3.1.3. Strategies for the Development of an Information Storage

Before developing an information storage, developing a balanced strategy that is appropriate for their needs and users it is important. Some questions, such as the following, are considered:

- Who is the audience?
- What is the scope?
- What type of information storage should be built?

There are strategies by which organizations can get information storage:

- 'Information storage virtual "environment, which is created by establishing:

- Installing a set of facilities for data access, directory, and management process.
- Training end-users.
- Control how information storage facilities are actually used.
- Based on current use, it creates physical information storage to support high-frequency orders.

- A copy of the operational data is constructed from a single operating system and enable the information storage a number of tools to access information. This strategy has the advantage of being simple and quick. If the existing data are of poor quality and/or access has not been previously evaluated, then a series of problems are created.
- Finally, the strategy information storage optimal number based on the value of the company and an analysis of their views, questions, and data access needs of users is selected.

According to these requirements, prototypes are built and information storage tested for end-user experience and modifies their requirements. Once a general consensus on the needs you have, the information comes from existing operational systems through the company and/or from external sources is obtained and loaded the information storage. If tools access to information is required, end-users are then allowed to have required permissions using their own favorite tools, or facilitates the creation of systems of access to multidimensional high-performance information using the core information storage base.

In conclusion, there is no single approach to build an information storage that suits the needs of enterprises, because these are different, like context. In addition, the information storage technology evolves; you learn more and more about the development of this and are that the only practical approach to data storage is the evolution of the person.

3.1.4. Strategies for Designing an Information Storage

The design of the information storage design is very different from traditional operating systems. The following points are considered:

- Users of information storage usually do not know much about the requirements and operational needs as users.
- Designing an information storage involves what you think in broader terms and concepts define business more difficult than

designing an operating system. In this regard, an information storage is fairly close to reengineering business processes.

- Finally, the ideal design strategy for information storage is from the outside in as opposed to top-down.

Although the information storage design is different from that used in traditional systems, it is no less important. The fact that end users have difficulty in defining what they need will not diminish priority. In practice, information storage designers use many "tricks" to help "visualize" requirements. Therefore, essential working prototypes.

3.1.5. Strategies for Management of Information Storage

The information storage requires careful marketing and management. The following strategies are considered:

- Information storage is a good investment only if end-users actually get faster and cheaper than current technology obtained with vital information. As a result, management has is seriously thinking about deposits for the effective performance they want and how to get to the end-users.
- Management recognizes that maintaining the structure of the information storage is as critical as any other application maintenance of mission-critical. In fact, experience shows that information storage has become one of the most used systems in any organization.
- The management also understands that if a program embarks information storage, new demands on their operating systems, which are created:
  - Demands for improved data.
  - Demands for consistent data.
  - Demands for different types of data.

3.2. THE DEVELOPMENT

3.2.1. Why Build Blocks of Information Storage?

To expand a business, it is necessary that the information is understandable. For many companies, this means a great information storage showing alongside the unfiltered data and scattered, creative new ways of presentation.

Tools that capture and explore evolve to detail and the ability to find ways to exploit the data collected. In recent years, two factors that help disseminate the information storage combined, these being:

- The benefits of online analytical processing (OLAP) are recognized beyond the traditional areas of marketing and finance. Organizations know that knowledge immersed in the masses routinely collect data about their customers, products, operations, and business activities, reduce operating costs, and increase revenues, not to mention that it is easier to make strategic decisions.
- The growth of the client/server creates hardware servers and more powerful and sophisticated than ever software. Servers today compete with mainframes offer yesterday and memory architectures technologically superior, high-speed processors and mass storage capabilities.

At the same time, base management systems (DBMS(s)) Modern, provide greater support for complex data structures. This renewal of hardware and software the information storage multi-terabyte (TB) now seen in environments client/server arise.

3.2.2. Preliminary Considerations for the Development of an Information Storage

There are many ways to develop information storage as many organizations exist. However, there are a number of different dimensions considered:

- Scope of information storage;
- Data redundancy;
- Type of end-user.

3.2.2.1. Scope of Information Storage

The scope of an information storage is as wide as all the strategic information of the company since its inception, or is as limited as personal information manager storage for one year. In practice, the broad scope, the greatest value of information storage is for the company and the most expensive and time-consuming is to create and maintain it. As a result, most organizations begin with information storage functional, department or division and then expand as users providing feedback.

3.2.2.2. Data Redundancy

There are three essential levels of data redundancy that companies consider in information storage options:

- Information storage "virtual" or "Point to Point";
- Information storage "central"; and
- Information storage "distributed."

You cannot think of a single approach. Each option adapts a specific set of requirements and a good strategy for data storage, is the inclusion of the three options.

1. **Information Storage "Virtual" or "Point to Point":** It means that end-users access databases directly operational data using any tool that enables "access network data." This approach provides flexibility as well as the minimum amount of redundant elements that must be loaded and maintained. In addition, unplanned loads consultation larger, are placed on operational systems.

As seen, the virtual storage is an initial strategy in organizations where there is a large (but mostly indefinite part) need to obtain operational data from a relatively large final class of users and where the probable frequency of orders is low. Virtual data warehouses provide a starting point for organizations to determine which end users are really looking for.

2. **Information Storage "Core":** It is the initial concept we have of information storage. It is a single physical database, which contains all data for a specific functional area, department, division, or company. They are selected usually where there is a common need of computer data and a large number of end-users and networked or mainframe. They may contain information for any specific period of time. These commonly contain multiple operating systems.

The information storage plants are real. The stored data are accessed from a place and loaded and maintained on a regular basis. Handlers are built around the advanced relational database (RDBMS) or, in some form of database server computer multidimensional data.

3. **Distributed Storage Information:** These are those in which certain components of the tank are distributed through a number of different physical databases. Increasingly, large organizations make decisions at lower levels of the organization and

simultaneously bringing the data needed to the local area network (LAN) or local computer that serves the decision-maker. Most involve redundancies and as a result, there are more complex update processes and cargo.

3.2.2.3. Type of End-User

In the same way that there are a lot of ways to organize an information storage, there is also an increasingly broad range of end-users.

Overall, we consider three broad categories:

- Executives and managers;
- "Users important" or "Buzo information" (financial and business analysts, engineers, etc.); and
- Users support (clerical, administrative, etc.).

Each of these different user categories has their own set of requirements for data access, flexibility, and ease of use.

3.2.3. Key Elements for Developing an Information Storage

The information storage successful start when choosing and successfully integrated three key elements. An information storage consists of server hardware and DBMS that make the deposit. On the hardware side, the configuration of server platforms combined, and takes advantage of the constant jumps of processor power. On the software side, the complexity and high cost of DBMSs is forcing to take drastic decisions and inevitable comparative balances with respect to integration, support requirements, performance, efficiency, and reliability.

If you choose incorrectly, the information storage becomes a large company with difficult problems to work in your environment, costly to fix and difficult to justify. For the implementation of the deposit have a successful start, it focuses on three key building blocks:

- Total storage architecture;
- Server architectures; and
- Management systems database.

Here are some recommendations to make the right choices for your company:

1. Architecture Design:

- **Deposit Architecture:** Information storage development begins with the logical and physical structure of the database of the deposit plus the services required operating and maintaining it. This choice leads to the selection of two key paragraphs: server hardware and DBMS. The physical platform is centralized in one location or distributed regionally, nationally or internationally. Then the following architectural alternatives exist:
  - A plan to store your company data, obtained from internal and external multiple sources, the database is consolidated in integrated information storage. The consolidated approach provides efficiency in both processing power and support costs.
  - The global architecture distributes information by function, with financial data on a server in a site, another marketing data, and manufacturing data in third place.
  - A tiered architecture highly summarized data stored on a user's workstation, with more detailed summaries on a second server and more detailed information on a third.

The workstation first level handles most requests for data, with a few passing on orders to levels 2 and 3 for resolution. Computers on the first level are optimized for users of heavy load and low data rate while other servers are more suitable levels and heavy volumes of data are processed, but lighter user load.

- **Server Architecture:** It is decided in a centralized structure or deposit distributed, they are considered servers that retain and deliver the data. The size of implementation (and business needs for scalability, availability, and system management) influences the choice of server architecture.
- **Single-Processor Servers:** Easier to administer, but offer limited processing power and scalability. In addition, a server only has a single point of failure, limiting the availability of deposit guaranteed.

You can extend a single network server using distributed architectures that use products, such as distributed computing environments (DCE) or broker architecture common object (CORBA), to distribute traffic across multiple servers.

These architectures increase availability, because the backup server operations are changed if a server fails, but management is more complex systems.

- **Symmetric Multiprocessing (SMP):** Machines SMP increase by adding processors sharing the internal memory of the servers and storage devices disk.

SMP most are purchased in minimum configurations (i.e., with two processors) and rise when necessary, justifying the growth processing needs. The scalability of an SMP machine reaches its limit in the maximum number supported by the connection mechanisms processors.

- **Massively Parallel Processing:** A processing machine massively parallel (MPP), a set of processors connected via a broadband link and high speed. Each node is a server, complete with its own processor (possibly SMP) and internal memory. To optimize an MPP architecture, applications are "parallelized" i.e., designed to operate separately, in parallel parts.

This architecture is ideal for searching large databases. However, the manager database (DBMS) that is selected is one that offers a parallel version. And even then, a design and essential attunement to obtain an optimal distribution of data and prevent "hot spots" or "data skew" (where a disproportionate amount of processing is changed to a processing node, due to the partition required data under its control).

- **Non-Uniform Memory Access (NUMA):** The difficulty of moving applications and DBMS environments to groups or parallel actually leads to new and emerging architectures, such as non-uniform memory access (NUMA). Creates a large SMP machine to connect multiple SMP nodes in one (although physically distributed) memory bank and a single instance of OS. It facilitates the SMP approach to get the performance benefits of large MPP machines (with 32 or more processors), while management advantages and simplicity of a standard SMP environment is maintained. Most important of all, it is that there DBMS and applications that can move from one processor or platform NUMA SMP unchanged.

2. **Management of Systems Databases:** The information storage (together with decision support systems (DSS) and client/server applications) is the first success for relational DBMS (RDBMS). Much of the operational systems are results based on old data

structures applications, warehouses, and DSS leverage the RDBMS for its flexibility and ability to consult with one specific goal.

RDBMS are very flexible when used with a standard data structure. In a standardized database, they are not redundant and represent the basic entities and relationships described by the data (for example products and trade sales transactions). But OLAP typical queries involving multiple structures, requires joint operations to place the data together.

The performance of traditional RDBMS is better for key queries based on content. To support large-scale deposits and to improve interest in OLAP applications, vendors have added new features to traditional RDBMS. These, also called super-relational, include support for hardware specialized base such as machine Teradata database data.

Supermodels support relational extensions to store formats and relational diagrams specialized operations and indexing. These techniques improve performance for recoveries based on the content, the pre-join tables using indexes or by using fully inverted index lists. Many of the tools access to information storage exploit the multidimensional nature of this. For example, marketing analysts looking at sales volumes per product, per market, per time period for promotions and announced levels and combinations of these aspects.

The structure of data in a traditional relational database data facilitates queries and analyzes along different dimensions that have become common. These schemes use multiple tables and indicators to simulate a multidimensional structure. Some products, implement storage techniques and operators that support multidimensional data structures. While multidimensional databases (MDDBs) directly help manipulate multidimensional objects (for example, easy rotation of these to view between different dimensions or movement operations successively exposed to more detailed levels) identified these when build the structure of the database. So, add a new dimension or change the desired view, it can be cumbersome and costly. Some MDDBs require a full reload of the database when restructuring occurs.

3. **New Dimensions:** One limitation of a RDBMS and MDDB is the lack of support for non-traditional data types such as images, documents, and video clips/audio. If these types of objects in an information storage are needed, it should seek an object-RDBMS. For its focus on values encoded data, most database systems to accommodate these types of information, only extensions based

on certain references such as indicators of files that contain them. Many RDBMS store complex data as binary large objects (BLOBs). In this format, they cannot be indexed, sorted, or sought by the server.

The object-RDBMS, on the other hand, store complex data as native objects and support large structures found in an object-oriented environment. These database systems naturally accommodate not only special types of information but also processing methods that are unique to each. But a disadvantage of the object-relational approach is that encapsulation of data within the special types, requires specialized operators to do simple searches previously. DBMS selection is also subject to server hardware used. RDBMS, provide versions that support parallel operations. The software divides parallel queries, connections across multiple processors and runs these operations simultaneously to improve performance. Parallelism for the best performance on large MPP and SMP clustered servers is required. It's not even an option with MDDBs or object-RDBMS.

4. **Combination of Architecture with the Management System Database:** To select the right combination of architecture and the DBMS server, you must first understand the business requirements of the company, the user population, and skills support staff. Implementations of information storage vary considerably according to the area. Some are designed to support the needs of specific analysis for a single department or functional area of an organization, such as finance, sales, or marketing. Other implementations gather data throughout the company to support a variety of user groups and functions. As a rule, a larger area of the tank, more power and functionality of the server and the DBMS it is required.

The models use the information storage is a factor. Consultation and reporting views are pre-structured to satisfy computer users, while there are fewer demands on the DBMS and server processing power. The complex analysis, which is typical of decision-support environments, requires more power and flexibility of all server components. Massive searches of large information storage favor parallelism in databases and servers.

Dynamic environments, with its ever-changing requirements, are better suited to architecture simple, easily changeable data (for example, a highly normalized relational), before an intricate structure that requires reconstruction after the change (for example, a multidimensional).

The value of fresh data indicates how important it is for the information storage to renew and change. Large volumes of these that are refreshed at frequent intervals, favor a physically centralized architecture to support efficient data capture and minimize transport time data.

A user profile should identify who the users of its information storage, where they are located, and how many bears are. Information on how each group expects to use the information storage helps in the analysis of the various styles of use. Knowing the physical location of users, helps determine how and what area needs to distribute the information storage. A tiered architecture server could use in place of LAN. Or you may need a centralized to support workers who are mobilized and working in the warehouse from their laptops approach.

The total number of users and connection models determine the size of deposit servers. Memory sizes and input channels and output (we/O) support the expected number of concurrent users under normal conditions, as well as the peak of their organization. Finally, the sophistication of support staff is factored. Resources information systems (IS) that are available within your organization, limiting the complexity or sophistication of server architecture. Without the internal specialized staff or outside consultants, it is difficult to create and successfully maintain parallelism architecture that requires the server platform.

5. **Expansion Plans:** As the deposit evolves and the data it contains are more accessible, external employees to deposit discover the value of information. By linking the information storage to other systems (both internal and external to the organization), information is shared with other business entities with little or no development. Mail messages, Web servers and intranet/internet connections, delivering lists tiered suppliers or according to condition business partners.

As the information storage grows in sophistication and uses the accumulated data within a company comes to be organized, interconnected, accessible, and generally available to more employees. The result is obtaining better decisions in business, work opportunities, and clarity.

3.2.4. Data Reliability

"Dirty" data are dangerous. No matter how the program is designed or how skillfully it is used. Unfortunately, the data used successfully in commercial online applications operating some are rubbish with respect to the information storage application.

"Dirty" data is presented to enter information into a data entry or other causes. Whatever, the dirty data damages the credibility of the implementation of the entire deposit. Fortunately, data cleansing tools are helpful. In some cases, an effective cleaning program is created. For large databases, inaccurate, and inconsistent data using commercial tools is almost mandatory.

Decide which tool to use is important and not only for the integrity of the data. If you make a mistake, you could waste weeks in programming resources and tooling costs.

- **Data Cleaning:** Cleaning dirty data is a multifaceted and complex process. The steps to follow are those:
  - Analysis of corporate data to discover inaccuracies, anomalies, and other problems.
  - Data transformation to ensure they are accurate and consistent.
  - Ensure referential integrity, that is the ability of information storage, to correctly identify instantly each business object, such as a product, a customer or employee.
  - Data validation that uses the application of information storage to perform the test queries.
  - Produce metadata, a description of the data type, format, and meaning related to the business of each field.
  - Finally, comes the crucial step of the entire process documentation so that it can expand, modify, and arrange the data in the future more easily.

In practice, multiple steps are performed as part of a single operation or when a tool is used. In particular, clean data and ensure referential integrity processes are interdependent. Commercial tools help in each of these. However, it is possible to write own programs to do the same job.

The data cleansing programs do not provide much reasoning, so companies need to manually make decisions based on relevant information and data audit reports. Each time it loads a new set of items, cleaning these commonly constitutes approximately 25% of which is a process of four weeks.

- **Types of Data Cleansing:**

- **Moderate Cleaning Data:** If you decide not to program data cleansing functions or hire a consultant to do the job, it can inhibit buying a specific tool for this task. Software information storage management is sufficient to clean and validate according to the purposes. Many projects using information storage products for various tasks information storage management, including:

1. Extracting data from operational databases.
2. Preparing to load data into a database repository.
3. Metadata management.

- **Data Intensive Cleaning:** For intensive cleaning work they are considered tools that are developed for these tasks.
- **Top-Down Approach:** This is an approach in which the client proposes rules to clean up the data. This is a direct approach, where knowledge about the business data is imposed.

For example:

- A series of concessions company X as a single client with multiple addresses are treated?
- For purposes of information storage, does it make sense to replace a single central management for different directions of concessions?
- It is preferred to treat the locations of concessions as completely different customers?
- This decision determines how to add or consolidates these records and if different addresses are treated as exceptions.

The main disadvantage of the top-down approach is that you have to know, or business rules and data cleansing are deducted.

- **Bottom-Up Approach:** This approach, analyzes the data and automatically emerge character models and business rules. It generally provides a design that normalizes these, conditions, and consolidates. This approach leaves few exceptions that are handled manually and the process consumes less time.

Like the top-down, approach takes into account the business relationships that are not obvious from the data, such as mergers and acquisitions taking place since the data were created. Impinges exclusively on cleaning the data, starting from the basic files. No extracts data from operational databases, load the data in the database warehouse, and synchronizes data duplicates or manages metadata.

3.2.5. Decisive Factors in Deciding the Development of an Information Storage

Dirty data is a serious threat to the success of a project of information storage. Depending on the extent of the problem, it is simply not possible to quickly steer it cheaper.

The main factors are:

- The time it takes the internal programming; and
- The cost of tools.

Project managers' information storage evaluates the problem realistically available domestic remedies that distribute and select the solution that adapts to the form and project budget or payroll and budget changes and the problem is solved.

3.2.6. Stages for Building an Information Storage

- ***Creating the Database Information Storage:*** After he identified the dimensions and key factors for the creation of information storage, a database denormalized which stores information is created that based on data from the actual database subsequently charged, then make the necessary consultations by of the generated queries information storage.
- **Types of Diagrams:** There are two types of diagrams that depicted or define the structure that performs the desired storage information for query information and not have limitations to existing standards in operating systems. These diagrams are known as:
  - Snowflake diagram; and
  - Star chart.
- **1. Snowflake Diagram:** It is an extension of a star diagram of one or more dimensions defined by multiple tables. A snowflake schema only joins the main table (fact table) primary dimensions. This diagram gets its name from the resulting image to add extensions hierarchical tables to chart stars.

For example the product hierarchy table. This is a brand, has a category and this one department (Figure 3.1).

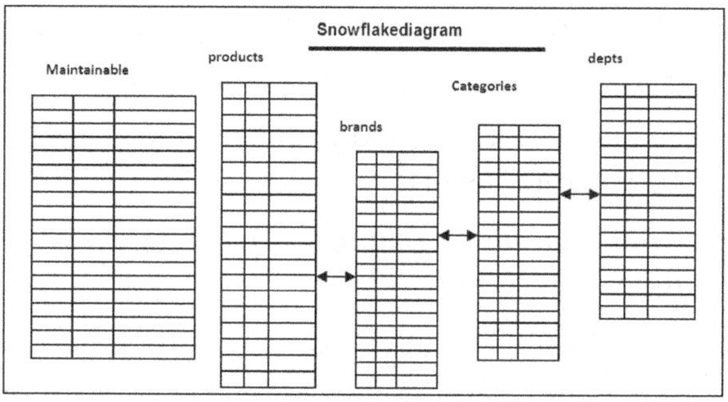

Figure 3.1. Snowflake diagram.

2. **Star Chart:** This diagram is used to solve problems that businesses have to a standard model.

- The center of the diagram is a table called "fact table" or main table containing key indicators identified during the analysis process and containing a combination of objects and time information. Indicators are the attributes and objects and the primary key times.
- In the surrounding area has dimensions that contain information objects and time.

The diagram star is implemented using technology relational database (Figure 3.2).

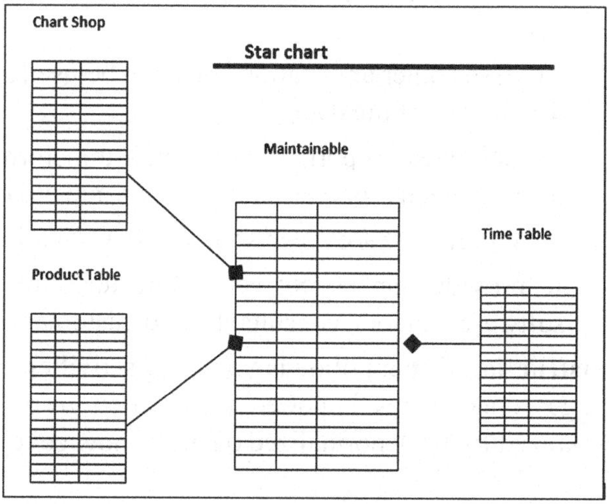

Figure 3.2. Star diagram.

i. Star Chart, Features Dimensions
   – Containing primary key.
   – Must have a one-to-many with the fact table.
   – It must contain at least one column descriptions.
   – Contain other attribute columns that are useful for the aggregation levels.
   – Contain a limited number of rows to slowly increase over time.

ii. Star Chart, Features Fact Table
   – It contains a primary key composed of foreign keys to the dimension tables.
   – It contains additional numeric columns.
   – You do not need to be any other combination of foreign keys.
   – It contains a large number of rows.

Continuing with the structure of information storage, the next step is the transformation of data.

- **Data Transformation:** For the transformation of the data a tool that facilitates this transformation is used and fulfills the following characteristics:
   – It is an application for consolidating data from a variety of heterogeneous sources and loads the data in the information storage.
   – Accesses other applications that can be used as a source or destination of the data.
   – It facilitates import, export, and transform data from heterogeneous sources not only the same environment.
   – It supports 100% of each source and destination of the data.
   – It provides an extensive architecture for independent software vendors, consultants, and customers.
- **Construction Cube:** Following building activities of information storage, since it has imported information from the database normalized to the denormalized database now cube is created.

As a cube definition, we say that is the central object data, which contains information on a multidimensional structure. Each cube is defined by a set of dimensions and measures.

- **Multidimensional Cube Structure:** Business information, you need to take the form of a question. The answer to these questions provides an input to the strategic direction of the business. Businesses need a multidimensional view to answer complex questions like:
  - What was the turnover of cherries in one place during the second quarter?
  - What product has the highest sales volume in each location during the fourth quarter?

There are many questions that are made without being based on measurements. This is where multidimensionality is not the first choice if the business asks questions that are not answered based on measurements. Some questions of this type are:

  - Who was the first employee hired during the first quarter of last year?
  - What products are added to inventory this year?

These questions are not answered with action. It is necessary to answer queries to access dimensional tables.

- **Building Dimensions:**
  - **Definition of Dimensions:** A dimension of a cube is a hierarchical view of information in the fact table or main table.

1. or The information is based on dimensional cubes.
2. or Using dimensions allows a drill-down analysis (starting at the highest level and down to detail level at level).

  - **Private Dimensions:** Private dimensions are those that are already created within a cube.

1. They defined at the time of the creation of the cube.
2. They are stored in the library of each cube.

  - **Shared Dimensions:** These dimensions are created independently of any particular cube.

1. They are stored in the information storage.
2. They are shared for one or more cubes.

3. They are used to standardize some business measures, to ensure consistency in several buckets.

- **Design and Construction of Aggregations:** Aggregations are pre-calculated data that enables the rapid response at the time of the query. Pre-calculated data server storing information for these calculations is recovered or makes any numerical calculation. The use of aggregations is the basis for a rapid response in OLAP systems.

Cubes are the way that aggregations are organized in OLAP systems. The dimensions mean the cube queries. Aggregations are stored at the intersection of the dimensions. Each intersection (called a cell) stores a single value.

To make an aggregation is considered essential both disk space and the explosion of data.

- **Cube Storage Methods:** The cubes are stored in multidimensional formats, a standard relational structure, or a combination of both. The storage method is chosen, influences the requirements and presentation of the cube. Within the cube, storage methods are the following:
  - ROAP (Relational online analytical processing).
  - MOAP (Multidimensional online analytical processing).
  - HOAP (Hybrid online analytical processing).

1. **ROAP:** It is a storage method that stores aggregations in relational tables, requires no extra space to store data, causes a slow response in comparison to MOAP consultations and HOAP. It is the best storage option for data that are often not consulted. Some of its features are:
   - Tables are created in an RDBMS.
   - Data loading is through INSERT INTO.
   - No data move OLAP server.
   - Indexes are created automatically.
   - It supports multiple database managers. (SQL Server, Oracle, Jet, ODBC).
2. **MOAP:** It is a storage method that saves data in a multidimensional structure. It offers the best performance in terms of consultations, because its structure contains data aggregations and base.

Consume plenty of storage space because cubes with many add-ons are too large.

3. **HOAP:** This is a combination of ROLAP and MOLAP. Aggregations are stored as the MOLAP structure. The data are based on relational tables. Queries that only they access pre-calculated data are as fast as the MOLAP structure. Queries that need to lose a lot of detail are slow as MOLAP structure but are quick as ROLAP structure. The HOLAP cubes are smaller than those MOLAP because of aggregations only stores and not on the data.

- **Process a Cube:** After creating the cube and defined aggregations, the bucket load is done with add-ons to the database. This is done by calling processes, which perform the complete loading of data. When a cube is processed, you call the store database and aggregations that are defined in these dimensions. Aggregations are then stored in the cube structure or relational databases. This process is time-consuming, based on the amounts of data and calculations (aggregations).

The information is updated in the following cases:

- When existing data is deleted;
- When aggregations are recalculated and stored;
- If the database has changed.

The cube can be used while it is being updated.

3.3. THE IMPLEMENTATION

At this stage, the draft information storage has assigned the right leadership, as well as human resources, technology, and the appropriate budget. However, other aspects such as the development of a project in whole or in phases and also differentiate the type of project carried out are evaluated.

3.3.1. Elements to Consider in Implementing

- **Total Project or Project Phases:** It is feasible to develop a project in phases that produce short-term results than the one that delivers results at the end of several years. Therefore, this should be centered in an area or process.

- **Logical Data Model:** You must have a higher reach and cover all areas of interest as well as the strategic processes of each. Example: the areas of marketing, credit, and marketing and segmentation processes, for record retention for credit and customer management, products, and sales channels are covered.
- **Specialized Project or Project Basis:** What kind of project is decided, it is somewhat complicated. One you specialized directly supports a specific process, for example, customer retention. One based delivery generic analysis capabilities to all users who have access to the information storage, but has, among its features, solving a specific problem, or specialized support such a process. A basic project is cheaper and easier to finish one specialized, more costly, and difficult to finish.

3.3.2. Strategies for the Implementation Process

For the implementation process, the following steps are defined:

- The problem in which the strategic use of detailed information, allows a solution to generate a competitive advantage or cost savings identified. Example: A problem may be the lack of a model for studies of customer retention.
- The logical data model is defined to be implemented to solve the problem posed. Example: You can give a model when it presents the user with information in terms of dimensions (customers, products, sales channels, promotions, acquirers, etc.) Basic model data and facts that are recorded for these dimensions (measurements sales, cost, production, billing, portfolio, quality, service, etc.).
- Data that populate the logical data model meet.
- Supplemental information initiatives that ensure the quality of the data required and the data model is completed are taken. These definitions are accompanied by an appropriate server for information storage and communications elements, client nodes, the manager of the database information storage and other hardware and software required for project implementation.

3.3.3. Implementation Strategies

The following are proposed:

- The best physical design for the data model defined. The physical design is aimed at generating good performance query processing, unlike which is user-oriented and ease of query logic model.
- Extraction processes, filter, processing load information and data that are implemented to populate the data model are defined.
- Processes information management remains in the information storage defined.
- Forms of consultations information storage information that is provided to the user. For this, we consider the need to solve a problem and the power of consultation.
- Query model based on the selected area is completed.
- Implement strategic processes work area, i.e., records deploy specialized tools, specialized tools for knowledge induction (data mining), etc.
- Complete areas of interest, similar to that described above.

3.4. EVALUATION

When costs are evaluated, the information storage user has no content costs in mind, but the minimum questions that begin to take are as follows:

- What kinds of costs exceeded the budget by more than 10% in each of the past 12 months?
- Are budgets increased by more than 5% for any area within the last 18 months?
- How to specify the kinds of expenses between different departments?
- How to have operating margins over the past two years in each business area? Where margins have declined, they are increased costs?

Often the really important issues identified by higher management, have an added value, which is known if they had the information he was looking for, which would mean an improvement, for example, sales by 0.5% to 1% – that if its operation was by the millions of quetzals in one year, resulting in hundreds of millions of queries. In some cases, the cost of the initial deposit is recovered over a period of 6 to 8 months. By asking questions of this type, users begin to identify areas where costs have increased or decreased significantly and can assess each of these areas in more detail.

Various costs and benefits in developing a project to build an information storage are identified, such as:

- **Costs:**
  - Preliminary costs:
  - Planning;
  - Design;
  - Modeling/engineering information.
  - Startup costs:
  - Hardware platform;
  - Database software;
  - Transfer tools and data cleansing.
  - Processing costs:
  - Data maintenance;
  - Applications development;
  - Training and support.
- • **Benefits:**
  - Tactical benefits:
  - Reduced printing and issuing report;
  - reduced demand for customer inquiries;
  - Faster delivery of information to users.
  - Strategic benefits (potential):
  - Access tools and applications for end-users;
  - More informed decisions;
  - Faster decision making;
  - Ability to support organizational information.

Benefits to be obtained are as follows:

- **For the Company:** The information storage makes it possible to harness the enormous potential value of the information resources of the company and potential return that value to true value.
- **For the Users:** The information storage extends the scope of information to be accessed directly online, which in turn contributes to their ability to operate more effectively or not routine tasks. Information storage users' access to a wealth of

multidimensional information presented cohesively as a single reliable source available to them through their workstations. Users use familiar tools, spreadsheets, word processors, and software for data analysis and statistical analysis to manipulate and evaluate the information obtained from the information storage.

- **Organization for Information Technology:** Information storage enhances the capabilities of the self-sufficient user and makes it feasible and offer new services to users without interfering with daily production applications. The constant struggle to meet the needs of users who request access to operational data, ends with the implementation of an information storage. Most users do not need to access more current data, because they have more useful information available from the information storage.

An information storage increases the value of investments in information technology, applications, and operational databases. How are you feeding information databases, to develop the information storage, become essential not only for daily operations but also as the source of business information of wide range?

CHAPTER 4

Software in an Information Storage

CONTENTS

4.1. QUERY AND REPORTING TOOLS

There is a lot of powerful query and reporting tools on the market. Some vendors offer products that allow more control over what query processing is done on the client and what the server. The simplest of these are products of this type. They provide from graphic displays (call access to databases or more accurate, generators) SQL generators.

More to learn SQL (structured query language) or write a program to access information from a database query tools like the visual majority, allow to target the menus and buttons to specify the data elements, conditions, grouping criteria and other attributes of an information request. Query tool generates then a call to a database, extracts relevant data, performs additional calculations, manipulates the data if necessary, and presents the results in a clear format.

Inquiries and orders report are stored for subsequent work as is or with modifications. The statistical processing is commonly limited to averages, sums, standard deviations, and other basic functions analysis. While capacities vary from one product to another, the query and reporting tools are most appropriate when you need to answer the question "What happened?" (Example: "How to compare sales of products X, Y, and Z last month with sales of this month and sales of the same month last year?").

To make consultations more accessible to non-technical users, there are products that provide graphical interfaces to select, drag, and drop. The most advanced of these consultations geared up with bad syntax or that return unexpected results. Access to data has also improved with new versions of these products and vendors already installed drivers (drivers) standards to commercial sources.

In general, managers information storage using these types of products, are willing to take their time to solve the tasks structuring and library management and directories, installing connectivity software, establish similar names in English and precompute "fields virtual data. "Once you have created the SQL screens, a set of query and reporting standards developed, although some products offer libraries of predesigned templates and predefined reports that can be changed quickly.

4.2. MULTIDIMENSIONAL DATABASE (MDDBS) TOOLS/OLAP DATA

Generators reports have limitations when end-users need more than one, a static view of the data, which are not subject to other manipulations. For these users, the tools of online analytical processing (OLAP) provide capabilities that answer "what happened?" when analyzing why the results are as they are.

The first solutions are based on OLAP multidimensional databases (MDDBs). A structural (twice a hypercube or multidimensional array) cube stores data to be handled intuitively and clearly see partnerships across multiple dimensions. The pioneer products directly support the different views and dimensional manipulations required by OLAP.

4.2.1. Limitations of the Approach of Multidimensional Databases (MDDBs)

- The new data storage structures require proprietary databases. There are really no standards available for accessing multidimensional data. Providers see this as an opportunity to create rules for editing APIs, promoting tools, and establishing strategic partnerships. Many of these query tools and data mining solutions directly support MDDB common formats. Some tools client/server are located on the top of a multidimensional information storage and support dynamic access and manipulation of data.
- The second limitation of MDDB concerns the development of a data structure. Companies often store data in enterprise relational databases, which means they are extracted, transformed, and loaded with this data in the hypercube. This process is complex and time-consuming, but again, providers are investigating how to solve them. Tools and other data extraction automate the process, mapping relational fields in the multidimensional structure and developing the MDDB on the fly.

Some vendors now offer technical relational OLAP (online analytical processing relational – ROLAP), which explores and operates in the information storage directly using SQL (structured query language) standard calls. Tools retain screens allow multi-dimensional orders, but the ROLAP engine transforms queries in SQL routines. Then the results tabulated as a multidimensional calculation sheet or otherwise supporting rotation and reduction are received.

As well as data extraction, development, and evolution of MDDB structure can be changed. ROLAP managers sometimes face tasks (overwhelming) to develop SQL routines to add ROLAP and index data as well as ensure the correct translation of multidimensional orders in the window SQL commands.

ROLAP advocates argue that open standards (SQL) are used and that (level of detail) are schematized data to make them more easily accessible. Moreover, they form a native multidimensional structure with better performance and flexibility, once the data store develops.

The good news is that these technologies are evolving rapidly and/or provide an early OLAP. Administrative and development of OLAP challenges unlike those found with query and reporting tools are generally more complex. Defining OLAP software and access to data, a clear understanding of the models of corporate data and analytical functions required by executives, managers, and other data analysts are required.

The development of commercial products ameliorates the problems, but rarely OLAP is a key solution. The architecture allows support to its source data and requirements. But once an OLAP system is established, the end-user support is minimal.

Users of these products decide whether data OLAP, to be stored in MDDBs specially designed or relational databases. This depends on the needs of the organization.

4.3. DATA MINING TOOLS

Data mining is a category query analysis tool. Instead of asking questions, they are taking and something "interesting" asks a trend or a peculiar group. This process extracts the stored knowledge or predictive information from the information storage without requiring specific requests or questions. It is a technology for end-user support, which extracts useful and usable knowledge from the information contained in the databases of companies.

The objectives are developed under the latest generation languages based on artificial intelligence (AI). The mining tools use some of the most advanced computing techniques such as:

- Neural networks;
- Deviation detection;

- Predictive modeling;
- Genetic programming.

To generate models and partnerships. Mining is a data-driven, not driven application. There are several different models of neural networks. Each of them has been designed for more or less specific purposes, however, there are several who have won great popularity.

4.3.1. The Kohonen Model

Before entering fully into the applications of ANN in the field of documentation we will stop briefly to analyze one of the models of the previous table most used in information retrieval, is the one developed by Teuvo Kohonen. At the beginning of the 1980s, Kohonen showed that information by itself, assuming its own structure and a functional description of the behavior of the network, was sufficient to force the formation of topological maps (Kohonen, 1982). These maps have the feature of organizing the input information by automatically sorting it.

This model has two variants:

1. The so-called "vector quantification of learning" (learning vector quantization) or LVQ, and
2. The so-called "topology-preserving map" or TPM. The latter is also commonly referred to as a "self-organizing map" (SOM). The difference between the two models is that while the LVQ works with outputs in a single dimension, the output in the SOM is two-dimensional. The latter is the most widespread.

The principle of operation of this model is simple; it is a matter of establishing a correspondence between the input information and a two-dimensional output space, or topological map. In this way, the input data with common features will activate areas near the map. It is very common to represent this network model with its output neurons arranged in a two-dimensional way, as we can see in Figure 4.1. When a data is entered into the network it reacts in such a way that only a neuron of the layer of output is activated. This neuron is called the winner-take-all unit and determines a point on the two-dimensional map. What the network is really doing is sorting the input information, since the winning neuron represents the class to which the input belongs, in addition to that before similar inputs the same neuron will always be activated. Therefore, the network is highly indicated to establish relations, unknown previously, between a certain set of data.

SOM model with its output neurons forming the map the learning method of the SOM model is called competitive and is of the unsupervised and off-line type, so it will have a previous stage of training and a later stage of operation. The Kohonen model is one of the most useful ANNs that have been developed, although it has two limitations: 1) the process of learning is often long and arduous, and 2) to learn new data it is necessary to repeat the learning process completely. However, the versatility of this type of network is very broad, allowing you to classify all types of information, from literary (Honkela, 1995) to economic (Kaski, 1995). Later they will be seen different applications of this model.

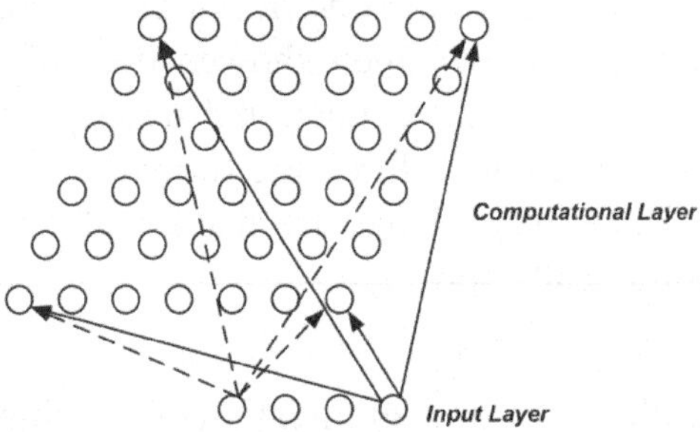

Figure 4.1. Network model with its output neurons arranged in a two-dimensional way.

4.4. ANN APPLIED TO THE FIELD OF SPECIALIZED LITERATURE

The topic of ANN is relatively new in the field of documentation and yet it has experienced a great boom in recent years. A study conducted in the library and information science database of abstracts (LISA), in its edition of winter 1996, allows us to observe the abrupt growth of the specialized literature in this subject. References were retrieved by searching for the term "neural" in free text, which yielded about 200 entries. From there, the entries corresponding to investigations in the course and only articles, reviews, and conference papers were left: 170 records. They were then ordered from time to time from 1981 to 1996, and the graph of Figure 4.2 was constructed. The exponential growth of the literature on the subject, especially in the periods 1992–93 and 1994–95. The fall of 1996 should not be taken into account since the information on this year is incomplete, which will be available in later editions.

Another important fact is the titles of journals involved in this study. Table 4.1 is listed out with the names of the publications ordered by their frequency of appearance. It is clear that this distribution resembles the one of the dispersion of Bradford, since it counts on a nucleus of few titles that monopolize a large percentage of articles while on the other hand, we have a large number of journals with only one or two articles (Figure 4.2).

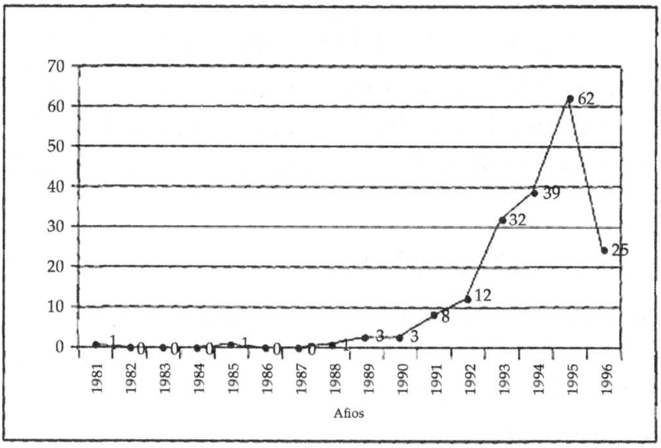

Figure 4.2. Articles on ANN in the base LISA.

The curious thing about the study may be that the most frequent publication is not specialized in neural networks or in AI, but comes from the chemical field. The journal of chemical information and computer sciences covers about 25% of the references on the subject, so we can say that the chemical information retrieval appears as the most active segment in the study of neural networks. Behind it appear different titles specialized in expert systems and AI, thematically more closely related to ANN, covering a range of 1.5 to 7.5% (experts systems 7.64%, knowledge-based systems 5.88%, IEEE expert 3.53%, AI review 2.94%, AI 1.76%). However, if we added the references of all these journals, we would not yet reach the numbers of the first. In the others we find titles of informatics in general (telematics and informatics 4.11%, Byte 2.35%), specializing in information retrieval and management 3.53%, information systems management (MIS) 1.76%, and library Hi-Tech 1.76), one specialized in biology and medicine (computer in biology and medicine 2.35%), and another in bibliometrics (scientometrics 2.94%). Behind them comes a platoon composed of 48 magazines that present at most a couple of articles about the theme.

The last issue that we must highlight is the fact that most of the titles specialized in documentation and retrieval of information, and which we could call the hardcore of the specialty, do not appear, or do so with one or two references. This would indicate that ANNs are not yet a topic fully addressed by the literature the discipline and that if we want to make a study about its application to the information retrieval we should pay close attention to the works that are in the border between diverse disciplines (Chemistry, Biology, AI, etc.) and documentation.

For a more in-depth study of the literature on neural networks, see the bibliometric Van Rann (Raan, 1993). It presents a map of science developed using the method of co-occurrence of terms in the thematic field.

4.5. APPLICATIONS OF ANN

ANN applications can be classified by various criteria. We will use an adaptation of the scheme of Scholtes (1995), which contemplates an ordering by type of application:

- Management of data;
- Classification of information (information clustering);
- Interface design;
- Information filtering;
- Incomplete searching;
- Information discovery (data mining).

The enumeration of applications is not intended to be exhaustive at any time, and the level of detail of each one varies depending on the information available.

4.5.1. Applications in Data Management and Data Mining

There are a few neural applications aimed at library management. Perez (1991) cites some, but all they are only packages aimed at accounting applications that have been used for forecasting budget in libraries. For Scholtes (1995), the experiences in this field focus on the management of loans and periodicals. However, it indicates that work in this field is increasingly rare. This is because it has been concluded that the information to be worked on is too precise and structured, whereas the optimal performance of ANNs is obtained with unstructured data and incomplete.

The automatic classification of information is the field where the most ANNs have been applied, particularly in the generation of two-dimensional maps of concepts.

As we have seen, one of the variants of the Kohonen model is that of self-organized maps by characteristics. Xia Lin, a researcher at the University of Kentucky and a specialist in the graphic representation of the information (Lin, 1991), uses these maps in order to generate a "displayable" output (map display) of a collection of documents (Lin, 1995, 1997). Lin presents three different examples:

1. A series of documents extracted from the INSPEC database through DIALOG,
2. A collection of personal documents, and
3. A group of papers from the SIGIR conference (1990–93). For each one of them, it generates a determined map through the following procedure:
   - A list containing all the terms appearing in titles and summaries of all documents of the collection.
   - Irrelevant terms are removed by a list of empty words (stop list).
   - A steaming algorithm is applied to the list to bring the terms to their root and reduce their number. Then duplicates are removed.
   - The terms with a high and low frequency of appearance are eliminated, preserving the middle zone of the spectrum.
   - A vector is created for each document of n dimensions, such that n is the number of terms that have remained on the list.

Each vector is completed with the weight associated with each term-document. The weight is calculated as proportional to the frequency of the term in the document and inverted to the frequency of the term throughout the collection. In some examples, the weights are dispensed with and only the presence or not of the term is indicated, through '1' and '0.'

These vectors are used as input to train a Kohonen network with n input elements (such as which is equal to the number of terms of each vector), and a variable number of outputs (e.g., 10x14 = 140 neurons), which will be the size of the output map.

This output map will also be represented by a vector of weights to which it is initially assigned small and random values.

During the training process, a random vector-document will be taken. The output neuron whose vector looks more like the vector-input document, it will be declared a winning neuron. Then the neurons (and those of their neighbors), will be adjusted to approximate vector-document.

This process is repeated for a number of cycles. When the training process has finalized each term is compared to the weights of the output neurons, in this way it is associated with the closest term (best-match term) to each of the outputs. Connecting the output neurons with similar associated terms will generate the different areas of the map.

With this output matrix, a map is constructed, and that corresponds to complementary visualization tools that can be added to the output map to obtain different resolution levels or pop-up menus for each node. The purpose of these add-ons is to facilitate the examination and visualization of the information represented on the map.

Lin establishes the limitations of the model, among which are: inability to work with high volumes of information and the high cost of information processing. However, the application of this model seems to be one of the most promising in automatic classification using neural networks. There are currently some applications that present a visualization map for internet nodes. On the subject, including a set of web pages classified by this method.

4.5.2. WEBSOM

On the same line as Xia Un has worked a finish group belonging to the Research Center in Neural Networks of the Technological University of Helsinki, directed by the own Teuvo Kohonen. The group developed by WEBSOM (Kaski, 1996; Honkela, 1996a, b; Largus, 1996), a system that allows automatic sorting large masses of information in full text, in order to facilitate their exploration and navigation.

The potential of this system has been demonstrated in a case study where group articles are organized. The treatment of this type of information is somewhat complicated due to that, unlike the maps of Xia Lin where formal information is organized (articles, presentations, patents, etc.), in Usenet groups are colloquial messages, without a specific format, usually with misspellings and no style correction (Figure 4.3).

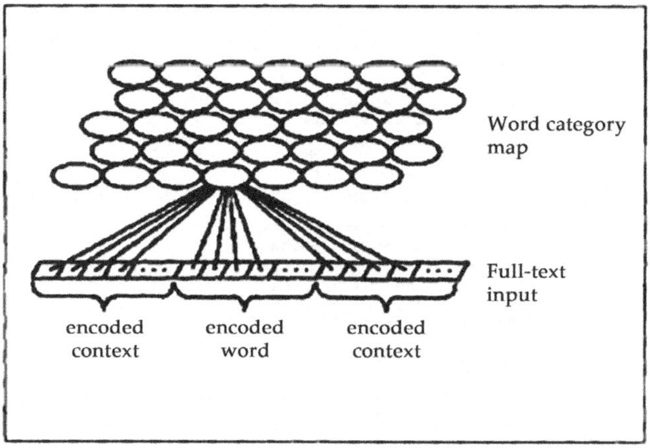

Figure 4.3. A grid of two dimensions with relations, such that words that tend to appear on the same node (or near one), form the same category.

Word category map represents a full-text input encoded context which contains about 1,200,000 words. To do this, it uses a method that consists of the following steps:

- Messages are taken and non-textual information is deleted. Special codes and numeric expressions are treated by heuristic rules.
- To reduce computational processing, we discard those words that have a low occurrence (Less than 50 times) and are treated as empty entries.
- In order to emphasize the theme of each message and reduce the erratic variations caused by different discussion styles, common words that make thematic discrimination difficult are eliminated. In the example of a total of 2,500, disappear 800.
- These words generate a first-word category map. These are ordered in a grid or map of two dimensions according to their relations, in such a way that words that tend to appear on the same node (or near one), form the same category (Figure 4.4).

This map is used as a histogram that filters information from documents. The authors define the histogram as the "fingerprint" of documents. With filtered and blurred information {Blurred), a second document map is generated, as can be seen in Figure 4.4.

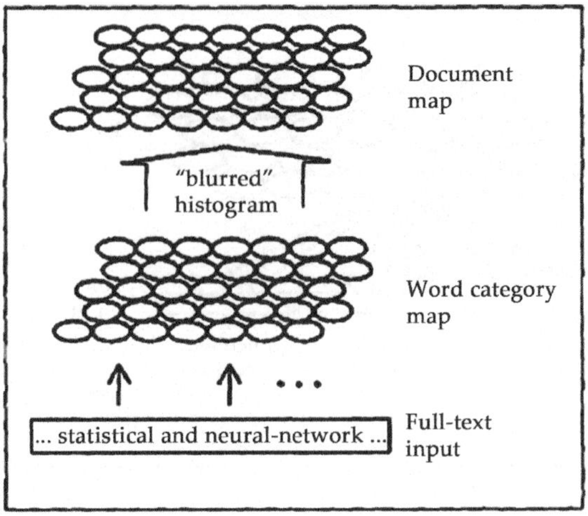

Figure 4.4. A second document map generated with filtered and blurred histograms.

In this way, the final product is a map like that of Figure 4.4, where each document occupies a place in the space according to its thematic contents. Each map area reflects specific content and topics vary slightly along the same. The different shades indicate the density of documents, the darker the more documents we will find.

The user interface to consult the map has not been neglected. This has been implemented in HTML and allows the exploration in four levels:

1. Global map;
2. Augmented zone;
3. Map of nodes; and
4. View of the message.

Level 1 presents a sensitive map with the whole of the documentary space. If we select a region of the same, it will appear enlarged in a similar map (level). At this level, it is also possible to "move" to neighboring areas without having to return to the general map and thanks to a tool that indicates with arrows the course to take. When we select a region this is the second map, we access a list of the messages or nodes of that region. It is also possible at this level like the arrows at level 2.

Finally, it is important to note that to generate these maps a great power of computation is needed.

In this direction, a public domain package for the simulation of LVQ networks is also available (Kohonen, 1996b). This is a prototype of a system of categorization of internet homepages. It has been developed by the AI Group of the University of Arizona, funded by several US government entities. The system tries to provide, automatically, and scalable, a thematic approach to categorization and search for information on the network. This project has analyzed the content of more than 110,000 homepages related to the field of entertainment. With this information, and using the Kohonen SOM model, a map of two levels with different thematic regions. In regions with more than 100 URLs, it is possible to access to a new, more detailed map. In the case of regions with less than 100 URLs, they are only accessed by a list of them. The map is constantly updated thanks to some splits or agents that they trace the network, in a similar way as the search services (Altavista, Lycos, etc.).

4.5.3. Maps of Scientific Publications Networks

A special application of the maps analyzed in the previous points is the organization of publications scientific research. The study of the relations between the different magazines of a certain thematic field is realized through analysis of the journal of citation report (JCR). This repertoire, published by the Institute of Scientific Information (ISI), collects quotations between different titles. This information is analyzed with different methodologies: cluster analysis, multidimensional scaling, principal component analysis, etc. Belltower proposes the study of these relations through the use of the Kohonen model (Campano, 1995).

Similar to the Lin procedure, a vector is constructed for each journal-title. The resulting vector has n elements, such that n is equal to the number of titles to be analyzed, and each element will contain the number of citations of each publication. The size of the output matrix is calculated according to the number of titles to be analyzed. Then the network is trained with the input information and a map called "map of relations », as can be seen in Figure 4.5a. In opposite, another map is obtained called the "domains map," and which represents only the neurons that are found the strongest response to a given journal (Figure 4.5b).

Only one title appears once on the map. Both maps are complementary and allow, through analysis of the size and proximity of areas, to study the relationships between two or more scientific journals.

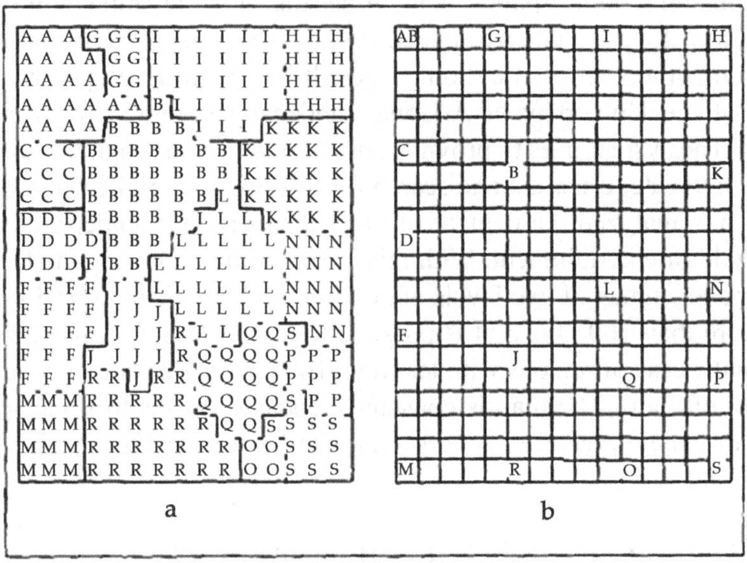

Figure 4.5. Map of relations and domains map.

4.5.4. Macleod's Algorithm

SOM is not the only method of neuronal clustering. Macleod has designed a specific algorithm for document clustering, using unsupervised learning (Macleod, 1991). In this work, the characteristics of the algorithm are analyzed and experimented through two small tests. Based on the results of these tests, it is demonstrated that the MacLeod algorithm is superior to hierarchical (sequential) clustering algorithms. Finally, it should be noted that the clustering is output independent of the order of entry of the documents.

4.5.5. ANLI: Adaptive Network Library Interface

ANLI is a program that acts as an interface between the user of an online catalog and the catalog itself (Kantor, 1993). The term network of the name refers to a network of relationships between documents, articulated through recommendations. These recommendations are provided by users and represent a certain value-added to catalog information. We can browse the network using a hyper-textual tool contained in ANLI, which allows different users to share information through "cooperative work computer-supported collaborative work (CSCW). The system is based, among other techniques, in neural networks, but unfortunately, Kantor does not go into detail about the nature and characteristics of the type used. It limits itself to saying that ANLI is a great "adaptive network" and that the neural model has been very useful in the overall development of the system.

4.5.6. Application in the Filtering of Information

Usenet newsgroups daily generate a volume of information that is impossible to assimilate. The secret in the use of these groups lies in the advance selection of groups and profiles of interest. Even so, the reading of this mass of messages is usually very arduous. To avoid this, Jennings, and Higuchi designed a system that filters Usenet information and is based on ANN (Jennings, 1992).

The operating principle of the system is quite simple, as can be seen in Figure 4.6. In the beginning, each article is analyzed to extract a series of relevant terms. These terms have associated a certain weight according to the place they occupy in the message (header, body, subject, etc.), and with them, the network of relationships is built. The terms of each new message are submitted to the network, if they keep any correspond to it, they will tend to activate or "trigger" certain nodes, and these, in turn, will be able to do so with others. In case the document generates certain activation, it is considered that it has the minimum energy to activate the network and is therefore accepted for reading. Otherwise, energy is not enough and therefore is discarded without being read.

The network is not maintained as a fixed structure, as it is modified by each input document. From similarly, with the passage of time non-activated nodes tend to lose weight, they may even disappear. This is to try to make the network dynamic and adapt to variations in the profile of the user with the passing weather.

Although this application is practical and interesting, Scholtes (1995) thinks that this system is not completely automatic, which is not adaptive and does not exploit the typical characteristics of ANN: generalization and association.

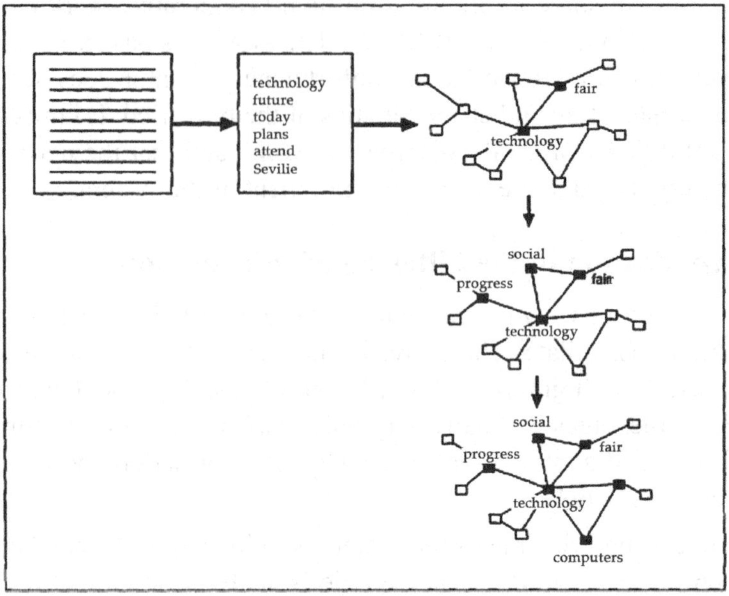

Figure 4.6. The operating principle of the system, where at the beginning, each article is analyzed to extract a series of relevant terms.

4.5.7. Incomplete Search Application within Neurodoc Project

The search and retrieval of information through natural language is a very important field of research. The degree of tolerance to typographical errors, the use of synonyms, etc., facilitates the human-machine relationship and makes this type of system open to a wide range of users. However, we cannot still talk about an anthropometric dialogue with the computer, because certain problems still exist not resolved. The main one is perhaps the inability of the system to supply the human interlocutor who, knowing of the nature and scope of the information contained in the database, allows guiding the user in the search of only that which can be found at the base. In order to provide an answer to this problem the Neurodoc Project has been developed, whose objective is to develop a recovery system that expansion of feedback questions (Lelu, 1991). The system is based on neural networks, although it clearly establishes the type of network topology used. A prototype of the system was programmed for the Macintosh environment (Lelu, 1992).

4.5.8. Intelligent Negotiation Neural Network (INN)

Research on information retrieval indicates that the search for topics is the most common and less satisfactory search modalities. In the same line as the previous system and with the in order to approach a solution to the problem of thematic recovery, the INN (Meghabghab, 1994). This system behaves as an information specialist capable of learning to negotiate the question of the user, in order to transform it into a correctly constructed search formulation and with greater possibilities of success.

The design of the INN is based on a multilayer ANN architecture using the backscattering algorithm (Back-propagation). A network called ACN (attentional connectionist network) is used for the separation of concepts, agents, and relationships, a knowledge base and analogical reasoning.

The network must be trained with at least 200 searches selected in advance. Once trained, the program is trained to intelligently process user questions. Meghabghab does not indicate any specific study on the performance of the system, but states that it significantly improves the percentage of hits for thematic search.

It is called data mining to study the recovery of information in adverse conditions (much noise, incomplete searches), and with various types of data (numbers, free text, structured records, etc.). As we have already stated, ANNs are extremely useful for the processing and search of heterogeneous information, incomplete, and with high levels of noise; So that these will find in the data mining an area of application which is very important (Scholtes, 1995).

This is a complete data mining package developed by integral solutions Ltd. A resemblance to so-called executive information systems (EIS). This product presents a series of advanced information processing tools, such as: rule induction, neural networks, regression models, information clustering using Kohonen networks, graphical analysis of information, etc.

Emphasis is placed on the fact that having a large amount of data does not guarantee obtaining the relevant information. This is also called data richness, information poverty. This is why the added value of information is the main objective of the program, and attempts to achieve it through the following functions:

- **Data Access:** The system can directly access the contents of various commercial databases, such as Oracle, Ingres, Sybase, and

Informix. You can import data from these databases and combine them with others from other applications, e.g., spreadsheets.

- **Data Manipulation:** It is possible to select records using a search criterion, and with them create a series of data that can be manipulated, exported, and processed.
- **Visualization of Data:** Information can be seen in different ways, such as histograms, clouds of points, distribution tables, networks of relations, etc. All presentations are interactive, being able to expand and reduce by zones.
- **Learning:** Through the neural networks and the induction of rules it is possible that the system "learns" make certain decisions without human supervision.
- **Visual Programming:** This is a complex program, however, it can handle with relative ease due to which any task is reduced to dragging icons and establishing visual relationships.

The system is not only addressed to the business world, but also to the scientist, and to any field where the decision making has a significant weight.

As we have seen in the present work, there are several applications that exploit the characteristics of ANNs and apply them to the field of information retrieval. However, they are still very large limitations. The main problem is the amount of information processing required. It is important to bear in mind here that ANN is a model of information processing, and that the systems that emulate them are just that: emulators of an ideal model.

This clarification is necessary in the case of ANNs, since most of the applications mentioned here simulate the operation of a massively parallel network using a sequential computer with Von Neumann's architecture. These simulations do not exploit the main feature of networks, parallel processing, making it impossible to develop applications that handle masses of real information. They are only limited to what Scholtes (1995) calls "toy problems."

The solution to this question is not to have more powerful sequential machines, but to have computers specifically designed for massive parallel computing, the application of the aforementioned method which has such a resource is the Kohonen WEBSOM.

Another issue to consider is the limitation of ANNs as to the nature of the information they can drive. The rise of these techniques may suggest that they are useful for solving information problems, but it is not like this.

The supremacy of ANNs is appreciated when it comes to processing information in the natural, noisy language and incomplete. In the context of information retrieval, it is common to see ANN applications to problems of structured information, which could be solved by other, more traditional methods that are easy to implement (Scholtes, 1995).

In spite of these limitations, ANN-based techniques applied to the retrieval of information often perform better than some other similar methods. The results from ANN are usually confronted with ones determined using the spectral polarization difference (SPD) method, as well as the HUT model-based iterative inversion. Generally, the results obtained using the ANN method are better than, or equal to results given using other techniques when trained with data that is previously simulated. Performances are also very good.

There are some obvious rules to follow when analysis tools are chosen. These are combined according to the needs of end-users, business technical capacity, and existing data sources.

- If a deposit provider also offers integrated tools you choose, you will probably save significant development time to choose a set that are compatible. Otherwise, a set that supports the original data source is selected. Without this, you should opt for a relational OLAP solution because it provides an open architecture.
- After you have selected a set of consistent tools with source data analysis it determines how much you really need.
- If you simply need to know "how much" or "many" will suffice a basic query and reporting tool.
- If you require more advanced analysis explaining the cause and effects of occurrences and trends, seek an OLAP solution.
- The Data Mining tools require sophisticated technical experts and data analysis needed for advanced forecasting, classification, and model creation.
- As with any technology, the best performance of the company opts for a single solution or set of solutions. Staff must understand the technology requirements, develop solutions that meet these requirements and effectively maintain and improve systems.

Intelligent business software is just a tool. Managers and executives who capture the derived knowledge and make decisions intuitively are still needed. In other words, these still require own business intelligence.

The parameters to consider in choosing the appropriate tools are defined in Table 4.1.

Table 4.1. Parameters to Consider in Choosing the Appropriate Tools

Tool Type	**Basic Question**	**Model Output**	**Typical User**
Consultation and reporting	What happened?	Monthly sales reports	Need historical data may have limited technical ability.
Online analytical processing (OLAP)	What happened and why?	Monthly sales vs. Price changes of competitors	You need to go from a static view of the data to a technically astute dynamic
Executive information system (SIE)	What do we need to know now?	E-books; Command centers	You need summary information or high level cannot be technically astute
Data mining	What is interesting? What could happen?	Predictive models	You need to remove the relationship and trends of technically astute unintelligible data.

CHAPTER 5

Artificial Intelligence and Its Impacts on Business

CONTENTS

5.1. BUSINESS PROCESSES AND BUSINESS DECISIONS

They are considering the potential business benefits of the following impacts:

- Process decision making are enhanced by the availability of information. Business decisions are made faster by more knowledgeable people.
- Business processes are optimized. Lost time waiting for information that is ultimately incorrect or not found, it is eliminated.
- Connections and dependencies between business processes are clear and understandable. Sequences are optimized business processes to gain efficiency and reduce costs.
- Processes and data from operational systems and data in the information storage, are used and examined. When the data is organized and structured to have business meaning, people learn a lot of information systems (IS). They are exposed defects in current applications, making it possible then to improve the quality of new applications.

Information storage just beginning to be consistent primary source of business information, the following impacts may begin to occur:

- People have more confidence in business decisions made. Both decision-makers and those affected know that it is based on good information.
- Business organizations and people that consist are determined by access to information. In this way, people are better enabled to understand their own roles and responsibilities as well as the impact of their contributions; at the same time develop a better understanding and appreciation of the contributions of others.
- Information sharing leads to a common language, common knowledge, and improving communication within the company. Trust and cooperation between different sectors of the company are improved, seeing reduced sectoring functions.
- Visibility, accessibility, and knowledge of the data produced greater confidence in operational systems.

5.2. TECHNICAL IMPACTS OF INFORMATION STORAGE

Considering the construction stages, the information storage support and operational support systems, have the following technical impacts:

- New skills development: When building the information storage, the largest impact on the technical people is given by the learning curve, many new skills must be learned, including:
- Information storage concepts and structure.
- The information storage introduces many new technologies (load, access data, metadata catalog, implementation of DSS/EIS), and changes the way that existing technology is used. Support new responsibilities, new demands, and new expectations resources, are the effects of these changes.
- Design and analysis skills where business requirements are not possible to define in a stable manner over time.
- They increase and development techniques are evolutionary.
- Cooperative teamwork with business people as active participants in the project.
- **New Operating Responsibilities:** Changes in operational systems and data are carefully examined to determine the impact these changes have on them and on the information storage.

Given the characteristics of the information storage system, the application has many uses in a variety of industries. However, generally speaking, it is said that its richest application is for enterprise environments where large data volumes associated with identified: number of customers, product variety, and number of transactions. Examples of typical applications are presented.

- **Retail Commerce:** In this trade, they use large massively parallel processing systems to access transactional months or years of history taken directly to the outlets of hundreds or thousands of branches. With this detailed information is made in more precise and efficient purchasing activities, pricing, inventory management, configuration gondolas, etc. Promotions and coupon offers are followed, analyzed, and corrected. Fads and trends are carefully managed in order to maximize profits and reduce inventory costs.

Existence is remapped by branches or regions according to sales and trends. These systems capable of processing a large amount of detailed data allow efficiently implement practices goods "on consignment," in this mode, the retailer pays the supplier only when products are sold and passed through the reader barcode (scanner) of point of sale. This detailed information allows exercise greater bargaining power over suppliers, since retail can get to know more than the manufacturer on the products: who buys it, where, when, with other products, etc.

Regularly what attracts an information storage is the kind of information obtained instantly. Anyone is chosen and tells exactly how much has been sold at a certain time, not on average, in every region, district, or branch. It makes it easier for providers to know more about your product. It provides a competitive advantage.

- **Manufacture of Consumer Goods:** Companies in this sector need to make an increasingly agile information management to stay competitive in the industry. The information storage used to predict the amount of product sold at a certain price and thus produce the right amount for a "just in time" delivery. In turn, the supply is coordinated large retail chains with huge quantities of goods "on consignment" which are not paid until these products are sold to the final consumer.

Retail chains and suppliers use the information storage to share information, allowing manufacturing companies to know the level of stock on the shelves and eventually take responsibility for the inventory replenishment retail chain. As expected, this strongly reduces intermediation. They are also used for marketing campaigns, planning advertising and promotions and coupon offers and promotions with retail chains are coordinated.

Major system applications are for marketing, sales, maintenance, warranty, and product design. It lets keep the existence of tighter parts and improve trading conditions with suppliers thereof.

- **Passenger and Cargo Transport:** Information storage is used to store and access months or years of customer data and reservation systems for marketing activities, capacity planning, monitoring earnings projections and analysis of sales and costs, quality programs and customer service.

Transport companies carry loads of historical data, of millions of shipments, capabilities, delivery times, costs, sales, margins, equipment, etc. The airlines use their information storage for frequent flyer programs to share information with manufacturers of ships, for delivery of freight transportation, shopping, and inventory management, etc. They keep track of spare parts, compliance with aviation regulations, supplier performance, baggage tracking, history bookings, sales, and refunds of tickets, telephone reservations, the performance of travel agencies, flight statistics, maintenance contracts, etc.

- **Telecommunications:** These companies use the information storage to operate in an increasingly competitive market, unregulated, and overall that, in turn, through profound technological change. Circuits, monthly bills, call volumes, services used, sold equipment, network configurations, etc.: data stored from millions of customers as well as billing information, utilities, and costs are used for purposes of marketing, accounting, government reports, inventory, purchasing, and network management.

Many other industries and activities currently use, or are beginning to install, information storage: government entities, especially for tax control, utilities, entertainment, publishing, automakers, oil companies and gas, pharmaceutical companies, drug stores, etc.

CHAPTER 6

Web Tracking System for Undergraduate College Career Based on Artificial Intelligence

CONTENTS

6.1. INFORMATION SYSTEMS (IS)

6.1.1. Definition

In the literature, there are several definitions of information systems (IS), which are targeted to specific types of issues on which we want to implement in this work. Below are four definitions of what an IS – is:

- An IS is a set of procedures, manual, and automated, and functions aimed at collecting, processing, testing, storage, retrieval, condensation, and distribution of information within an organization aimed at promoting the flow of them from the point generated to the final recipient of the same (Rodriguez and Daureo, 2003, p. 29).
- An IS can be defined as a related and connected software components and hardware that are used to collect or recover, and then process and store, and finally distributing the information set (Shipsey, 2010, p. 6).
- An IS is a set of interrelated components that collect, manipulate, store, and distribute data and information and provide feedback mechanisms to accomplish a goal (Stair and Reynolds, 2012, p. 4).
- An IS is a set of elements that interact with each other in order to support the activities of a company or business (Antonino and Martin, 2014, p. 2).

From these definitions, it abstracted that an IS is a related software and hardware set, which works to collect, store, process, and display information to the user. In this paper we shall refer to the latter definition, which is the most general, taking the nuances of the first, which deals in more detail the computational form of IS.

More specifically, the concepts of knowledge, information, and data are used often in this area and are often treated as the same concept, but it is necessary to define and distinguish each of them in particular and the way in which they relate (see Figure 6.1), as is done in (Stair and Reynolds, 2012, p. 5):

- **Fact:** The data consists of raw facts, such as the number of an employee, the total number of hours worked in a week, the number of items in inventory or sales orders.
- **Information:** A collection of facts organized in a way that has added value beyond the individual value of the facts.
- **Knowledge:** Understanding and awareness of a set of information and ways this information can be useful to support or reach a specific decision.

The IS consists of three functions which are key to its operation (Shipsey, 2010, Stair and Reynolds, 2012, Antonino and Martin, 2014, Rodriguez and Daureo, 2003) and its components relate to each other, where:

- **Entry:** It is defined as the activity of collecting and capturing information from real-world data that the system requires. Entries can be given manually or automatically, where the manually indicates that the user directly supplies the information and the control the data or information are obtained from other systems or other processes.
- **Processing:** In IS, the processing is related to the conversion or transformation of input data into information. This process may involve sorting, calculations, and formatting changes, among others.
- **Departure:** This function is responsible for the information that was processed is shown to users, who will use this information for purposes they deem (for example as an aid to decision making). The output information can be presented by various means; including the output of a system can be the input for another.

6.1.2. Types and Characteristics of Information Systems (IS)

As O'Brien and Marakas say (2009) "In theory, IS implemented in the business world today can be classified in different ways, "then the different types and subtypes of IS that are currently (Figure 6.1) are presented.

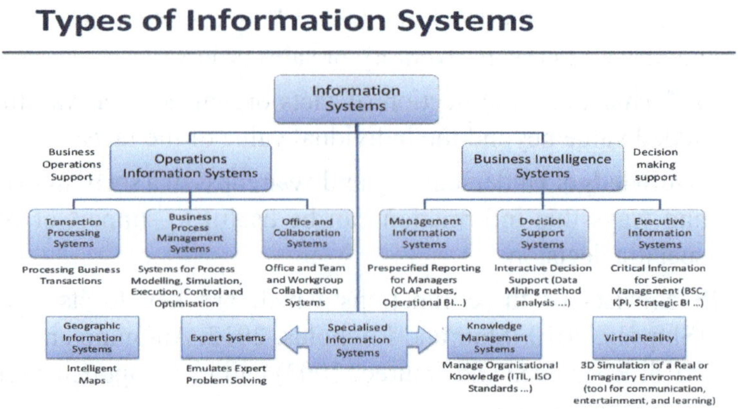

Figure 6.1. Types of information systems.

Source: Singidunum.

In the context of this work, the guys who want to analyze correspond to (Antonino and Martin, 2014):

- Transactional systems:
  - Automate operational tasks of the organization;
  - It is usually one of the first IF to be incorporated in organizations (part from the bottom and evolves as time passes to make increasingly complex and important tasks);
  - They require a lot of data management for their operations and generate large volumes of information.
- Systems decision support:
  - The information generated provides support for decision-making;
  - They are few inputs and outputs, but the process with lots of calculations;
  - Are IS with high standards of graphic design, as it is aimed at end-users.
- Strategic systems:
  - They can automate processes and help decision making;
  - Its function is to achieve benefits that competitors do not have, are creators of barriers to entry business;

- They help the process of innovation of products and processes as they seek advantages over the competition.

6.1.3. Applications

As indicated in the literature there are several types of IS, each created to perform a particular task, such as mentioned Valacich and Schneider (2011, p. 30) "Your local store uses transactional systems in the box, which scans the bar codes of the products. Every hour, the online retail website processes thousands of transactions amazon.com around the world ," which shows that rates if you have particular applications in the context of these book applications of interest are:

- Academic management software for universities.
- Software for academic administration and management.
- Academic IS.
- Institutional academic IS SINAI.
- Moodle.

6.2. EXPERT SYSTEMS

6.2.1. Definition

Expert systems belong to the field of artificial intelligence (AI) and are the part of it that most field has occurred in the commercial sector, its name derived from the term "expert system based on knowledge," therefore, and as described in (Quintana, 2007). Generally, an expert system is an interactive computer program containing the experience, knowledge, and own ability of a person or group of persons skilled in the joint area of human knowledge, so as to resolve problems specific to that area intelligently and satisfactory.

These systems mimic the reasoning processes used by experts to solve a specific problem, however, this imitation depends on the quality of the design of such a system, sometimes these systems can work even better than their human counterparts, making decisions in a specific area called domain.

In what concerns the implementation of this work the definition proposed by Engin and the company used (Engin et al., 2014), where it is defined and delivered characteristics of a rule-based expert system: "The rule-based expert systems have the ability to emulate the decision making of human experts. They are designed to solve problems as humans do, exploiting the codification of human knowledge. This knowledge can be extracted or purchased directly from interaction with humans, as well as from printed or electronic, such as books, magazines, or websites resources. The extracted knowledge is the basis of knowledge of the rules-based system."

It is noteworthy that the development of this project is not an expert system that will be implemented, but some of its main features in order to design a hybrid system that allows solving the problems addressed be taken.

6.2.2. Features an Expert System

First, it should be noted that, since the "knowledge" of an expert system comes directly from a human expert, this should represent that knowledge in order to solve problems, justify their behavior, and be able to incorporate new knowledge.

The SE is composed of two main parts: the development environment consultation and the environment. The development environment is used by the constructor to create the components and introduce knowledge in the knowledge base. The consultation room is used by non-experts to obtain expert advice and (Badaro, Ibañez, and Aguero, 2013, p. 6) knowledge.

The following are the basic components of a SE:

- **Knowledge Acquisition Subsystem:** It is the accumulation, transfer, and transformation of experience to solve a source of knowledge to a computer program to build or expand the knowledge base.
- **Knowledge Base:** Contains the necessary understanding, knowledge formulate and solve problems. It includes two basic elements: special heuristics and rules that guide the use of knowledge to solve specific problems in a particular domain.
- **Factual Basis:** It is a working memory containing the facts about a problem, it houses the corresponding own data to the problems that you want to try, or is a part of memory the computer that is used to store data received initially for resolution a problem.
- **Inference Engine:** It is the brain of the SE, also known as control structure or rule interpreter. This component is essentially a computer program that provides reasoning methodologies for information in the knowledge base. This

component provides directions on how to use knowledge of the system to arm the agenda that organizes and controls the steps to resolve the problem when a query is made. Has three main elements: (1) Interpreter, executes the selected agenda; (2) scheduler maintains control over the agenda; (3) consistency control attempts to maintain a consistent representation of the solutions.

- **Subsystem Module Justification or Explanation:** It is responsible for explaining the behavior of the SE to find a solution. It allows the user to ask the system to understand the lines of reasoning that this continued. It is especially beneficial to non-expert users looking to learn how to perform some kind of task is valuable, especially to those users who must base their decision-making, depending on what offers the SE.
- **User Interface:** It allows the user to describe the problem expert system. Interpret your questions, commands, and information offered. Conversely, it makes the information generated by the system including answers to questions, explanations, and justifications. That is, enables the response provided by the system is intelligible to the person concerned.

It is noteworthy that the development of this project is not an expert system that will be implemented, but some of its main features in order to design a hybrid system that allows solving the problems addressed be taken. Based on the above facts alone base or database will be taken into account, certain properties module explanation and user interface.

6.2.3. Applications

Most companies have the technological infrastructure to support basic functions of information processing: general accounting, financial decisions, treasury management, planning, etc. In this regard, expert systems are applied in a variety of fields and/or areas, for example, IT, telecommunications, electronics, education, finance, and management.

What matters for the development of this project are the applications in the areas of education and management, and in this context some examples.

In (Engin et al., 2014) the authors, propose two expert systems for student Support University undergraduate. Where the first is a system that advises courses, suggesting undergraduate students; while the second system suggests scholarships to undergraduate students, based on eligibility.

6.3. MONITORING INFORMATION SYSTEMS (IS)

6.3.1. Definition

Before detailing that is a tracking system, you must know the context in which the word is used, monitoring refers to the control application, periodically, to variables or indicators to use, generate information from the changes they undergo in a given time, due to support decision-making, management support of a system of any type (business, education, etc.) and provide quality product. That said, since a system not only involves software implementation, but it contains all the characters who are actively involved in this, the International Organization for Standardization (ISO acronym in English), presents a set of rules determining that must contain a system that grants provided to the product quality and ensure consistent customer satisfaction as to what this system provides. Therefore, the overall development of these systems is required (p.2):

1. Determine the processes needed for the system and how they are applied;
2. Determine the sequence and how processes interact;
3. Determine criteria and methods needed to ensure that both the operation and control of these processes are effective;
4. Ensure the availability of resources and information necessary to support the operation and monitoring of these processes;
5. Monitor, measure where applicable and analyze these processes;
6. Implement actions necessary to achieve planned results and continual improvement of these processes.

Those who use this system should implement the above requirements, in order to:

1. Demonstrate conformity to product requirements;
2. Ensure system compliance; and
3. Continuously improve the efficiency of the system.

Therefore, a tracking system is one that uses the information it contains, and complies with established standards, in order to provide quality international standards, the management of the problem for which it was developed.

6.3.2. Features of a Tracking System

To ensure product quality ISO proposes a number of criteria that must be met to provide a degree of quality, it is in this sense that a monitoring system must comply with the characteristics set out in point "8.2 Monitoring and Measurement" (p. 12), as a guarantee this quality. Therefore, the characteristics to be met are as follows:

1. ***Customer Satisfaction*:** As a measure of system performance, you should track information relating to customer perception regarding compliance with the requirements.
2. ***Internal Audit*:** Must conduct internal audits within ranges previously stipulated, due to determine if the system meets the planned arrangements, if it complies with the international standard and if you meet the system requirements established, in addition to determining whether the program has been implemented and it is maintained effectively.
3. ***Monitoring and Measurement of Processes*:** Suitable methods should be applied for monitoring in order to demonstrate the ability of the processes to achieve results that were planned. Not achieve results, should carry out corrections and corrective actions.
4. ***Monitoring and Measurement of the Product*:** They should carry out monitoring and measuring the characteristics of the product, in this case, a system of tracking information to verify that its requirements are met.

Since the proposed solution to the problem is the implementation of an IS monitoring it is important to properly deal with the last two points in particular. That said, it should be added that along with determining which process monitoring will be done, determine what aspects of this are to be controlled, and more importantly, that indicator(s) will be associated with the process. It should be noted the importance of correctly associate each indicator as these that will determine whether the planned results have been achieved or not.

6.3.3. Applications and Functionalities

According to what is stated in ISO: 2008, requirements to comply can be associated with any organization, regardless of type, size or product provided.

However, by way of exemplifying how these systems are used in the area of education, the following examples are:

- In (Yamasato, 2006) planning to implement a "system monitoring, analysis, and evaluation of medium-term plans" is performed, which aims to facilitate the process of monitoring the actions of the Peruvian government education sector, so as to allow make corresponding assessments improve the planning process the Ministry of education (p. 6). To achieve this objective the author conducts research in the education sector, on the basis educational roles of the state, proposed in the constitution of that country, in order to identify gaps in planning education strategies, so that it can use this information to develop a monitoring system so as to solve these shortcomings.
- In the following example, the Central University of Ecuador presents the design and development planning of a "monitoring and control system for the improvement plan" (Central University of Ecuador, 2014), which main objective is to provide regular, timely, and reliable information, which relates to the implementation of the activities of the university, fulfilling goals and indicators of the plan, implementation of the allocated budget and compliance with established schedules, in supporting decision making and corrective processes related to the implementation of the plan. For this, the system has a series of characteristics, which are: Using the platform Cloud Google (Google Docs and Google Drive, for example), processing of information on the progress in implementing the activities, the processing performed by Google Docs spreadsheets, among many others.

6.4. QUALITY INDICATORS FOR HIGHER EDUCATION

6.4.1. Initial Indicator

In general, there is no official definition as they are indicators, however, there are some references, as expounded by A. Mondragon (2002): "tools to clarify and define more precisely, objectives, and impacts (…) are verifiable measures of changes or results (…) designed to have a standard against which to evaluate estimate or demonstrate progress (…) to set targets, facilitate the distribution of inputs, producing (…) products and achieving objectives (United Nations Organization (UN), 1999). The author also cites the definition made by Bauer in 1996 (Horn, 1993), which is defined indicators as "(…) statistics, statistical series or any kind of indication that facilitates us to study where we are and where we are headed with respect to certain objectives and goals and to evaluate specific programs and determine their impact (…)."

Indicators can be qualitative and quantitative. When it is necessary to prove a career, it is imperative to meet the criteria proposed by the National Accreditation Commission, therefore, if you want to establish educational quality and management of this race, you need to track the explicit and implicit in each of the criteria of these documents indicators.

Here are three documents prepared and designed by the NAC, which comprise evaluation criteria for professional careers in general engineering careers and finally undergraduate careers are summarized.

The following document establishes the NAC 9 general evaluation criteria (CNA, National Accreditation Commission, 2007), which are broken down between mandatory criteria (must) and criteria recommended (should) criteria that have been established generally for any professional career, regardless of the category of these.

Compiling possibly the most important of each of these aspects criteria set out below:

1. ***Purposes***: The criterion is defined in terms of, as mentioned in the statement, the purpose of the race, which must be in sync with the unit (University, CFT, Professional Institute, etc.) must be clearly defined, and the ability to be checked periodically. Turn the unit should clearly define the competences of the profile expected for students exit, however, if this leads to a professional

qualification grade graduation, this must be justified in the skills of the graduate profile.

Finally, the unit must demonstrate that it has and implements mechanisms for periodic evaluation of the mission, goals, and career objectives.

2. ***Integrity***: The criterion indicates that the unit must provide full, clear, and realistic those who use their services, while respecting the conditions of teaching their students to enroll information. In addition, as an important point, the unit must take care that there is an appropriate balance between the number of students entering each year and the total resources available to the program. Generally, the unit must be clear in the delivery of information, which should be freely available, should also constantly improve the internal regulations of each race, and widely spread among students, along with the rights of these.
3. ***Organizational, Administrative, and Financial Structure***: The criterion defines the organizational requirements that must be the race, which must demonstrate that it has an adequate system of governance and an effective institutional, administrative, and financial management, which should aim at improving through ongoing assessment processes. In this evaluation, the process should be used instruments for progress and strengthening of self-regulatory capacity.

On the other hand, there must be mechanisms of communication and IS to facilitate the coordination of its members.

Finally, with respect to funding, it should ensure financial stability, and should include at least adequate planning and effective budget control mechanisms.

4. ***Curricular Structure***: Criterion which is part of the structure of the curriculum of the race, which should be based on the student's graduate profile, considering both the skills directly related to job performance, such as general and complementary. Curricular programs such as structure must integrate both theoretical and practical activities, so that students experience in fieldwork is guaranteed. Thus should provide instances of connection with the external environment through activities such as technical visits and related practices.

As is defined in each of the criteria, there must be mechanisms to regularly evaluate the curriculum and programs. However, it is proposed that in this particular case, the evaluation should consider internal and external opinions, academics, students, graduates, employers, and others.

Finally, it must be ensured that vocational training is carried out in an atmosphere of intellectual development and own personnel of an academic community.

5. ***Human Resources (p. 7):*** Perhaps one of the most important criteria for university education is the one that has to do with who impart knowledge to do the NAC indicates that it must show that the unit has an academic staffing adequate in number, dedication, and qualifications to cover all functions defined in its purpose.

The unit must have both teachers and technically trained, sufficient in number and time dedicated administrative staff, and appropriate support to fulfill their duties properly. The suitability of the faculty should be established taking into consideration the training received.

The unit must have a system of teacher training that allows updating their academic both pedagogical aspects and the proper disciplinary and professional, and to encourage teachers to engage in teaching, research, technological development or other that arising from its institutional project.

Finally, there must be mechanisms for the evaluation and development of teaching, mechanisms should consider student opinion.

6. ***Effective Teaching and Learning Process*:** The criterion establishes the rules to be followed to determine the effectiveness of the learning process, is quoted: "The unit must have clearly established criteria, public admission and appropriate to the needs of their curriculum. The teaching process should take into account the skills of students and the requirements of the curriculum, providing opportunities for learning theoretical and practical, as appropriate. The unit must show that the evaluation mechanisms applied to allow students to check the achievement of the objectives outlined in the curriculum."

It must constantly perform analysis of the causes of dropout students and define actions that tend to diminish the situation. A turn should develop mechanisms for academic counseling or mentoring, so that the academic performance of students is monitored throughout the race, applying the actions or measures necessary.

7. ***Results of the Training Process*:** The main criterion defines the actions that should or should then take the exit of students. Track

retention rates, approval, titling, etc., as well as track their own graduates.

The unit should consult employers or users of professionals trained in the race and use all backgrounds in terms of improving, updating, and refining the plans and programs of study.

8. ***Infrastructure, Technical Support, and Resources for Teaching:*** The criteria essentially define the structural conditions, techniques, and resources aimed at teaching the unit must provide to suit their purposes fully to achieve the expected learning outcomes and meet your development project. These resources should be appropriate in number, quality, and condition. In addition, it must be demonstrated that the teaching process makes frequent and proper use of technical and infrastructural resources.
9. ***Connectedness***: The last of the criteria referred to links with the disciplinary and professional fields that the unit must ensure this in order to update the knowledge imparted.

It is suggested to identify, understand, and analyze its significant environmental and consider such information towards the planning of activities. Finally, in all cases, he cited: "(...) The unit should define a policy face and explicit to enable it to plan, organize, and develop the activities you choose to perform, allocating resources of all kinds necessary."

6.4.2. Criteria for Engineering Careers

As mentioned in the previous section, NAC proposes 9 criteria to determine and provide the degree of accreditation requested by a career in general, however, there are modifications or variations of these criteria that help define the specific conditions to be met a race higher education to achieve this degree, in this case, the particular criteria for engineering courses and degrees are addressed in the current section and the next, respectively, focusing mainly on the differences they possess against general document detailed in section above.

6.4.3. Criteria for Undergraduate Careers

Indicators for undergraduate careers usually shared nine indicators that have careers, guiding them to their requirements. As discussed in section 6.4.1, there is a greater degree of specification in the point 4 (i.e., curriculum structure), point 6 (i.e., effective process learning), and point 9 (i.e., connectedness), which are shown below:

The curricular structure incorporates the following criteria:

The unit should ensure that licensed training is conducted in an atmosphere of intellectual development and own personnel of an academic community in which attitudes or behaviors related to develop:

1. **Training and Ethical Consistency:** Ability to assume ethical principles and respect the other, as a rule of social coexistence.
2. **Integral Formation:** Ability to understand the interdependent aspects of the globalized world.
3. **Citizen Education:** Ability to integrate into the community and responsible participation in civic life.
4. **Aesthetic Judgment:** Ability to assess and evaluate various artistic, cultural, and contexts from which they come expressions.
5. **Environmental Awareness:** Ability to understand the problems and challenges involving the protection of the natural and urban environment, and acting responsibly towards them.

Effective teaching and learning process incorporates the following criteria:

- The unit must have expeditious mechanisms of communication with their students.

Connectedness incorporates the following criteria:

- The unit must have an explicit policy to promote links with the disciplinary through their academics, indicating the activities considered in the policy, the mechanisms for access to, the resources are allocated and how they will be considered in the academic evaluation.
- The unit should consider various forms of linkage with socio-cultural, artistic, productive or service sectors that are related.
- If the unit develops service delivery activities, these should be organized clearly and explicitly, not to interfere with the priority tasks of the race.

6.5. WEB METHODOLOGIES

In this chapter different aspects were addressed, both websites and web applications; detailing how most web applications and their importance.

Usually, people confuse a website with a website, but we must make a distinction between these two terms, which despite being related are not the same. "A website is a set of web pages related. It is understood by the website both the file containing the HTML code as all resources used on the page (images, sounds, etc.) ," from the above it is concluded that a website is a component of a website.

Currently, there are a variety of websites, each oriented to a specific category, such as Tarafdar and Zhang say (2005–2006) "Websites serve different purposes, shop, gather information, entertainment, research, and others. So there are different categories of websites." These authors also explicit that "The relative importance of the characteristics of a web site varies, depending on the domain to which the website belongs." That said, you can identify that there are different categories of websites, each associated with domains and different needs, this makes it difficult to reach a consensus on what are the general features that should have a website, but if you are of according to the features that should have a website to be considered good for the user, according to Zhang and Tarafdar (2005–2006) and Ahmed Al-Salebi (2010) These features are:

- **Visual Design:** It must be well designed to draw the user's attention. There are five criteria on visual design a website should consider, which include page layout, navigation, and consistency, include images, appropriate use of colors.
- **Readability:** The website should be human-readable, readable websites give a quick user who does not decide whether to stay or impact. There are three criteria that help a website is readable and understandable, these are: The font size, font type, and font color.
- **Content:** A website should have content and that is the purpose of creating it; It must make sense to the user, so the content should be related to the purpose for which the website was created. The content must have the following characteristics: The information must be relevant for the purpose of having a website, easy to read and understand, useful, you must have adequate scope and depth, and must be current.
- **Technical Properties:** There are some technical features on websites to consider, which are: Security, whose security features are determined by provisions for user authentication and secure

transactions; access speed, accessibility, and availability of the website.

Regarding the architecture of the web sites, literature are different types of network architecture, according to Kurose and Ross authors architectures that predominate are the client-server architecture and peer-to-peer (P2P) architecture. For the development of this book is chosen by the client-server architecture, which is defined as: "A customer is a program running on a terminal that requests and receives a service from a server program running on another terminal" (Kurose and Ross, 2009, p. 12), this is a broad definition of how this architecture, which the authors complement indicating works. "In the client-server architecture, there is an always-on host, called the server, which receives requests, many other hosts, called clients. It should be noted that the client-server architecture, clients do not communicate directly with each other "(p. 88).

In the literature there are several definitions of web applications within them including the following:

- "A web application is an application that is designed from the start to run in a web environment."
- "Web applications are client-server applications in which a web browser provides the user interface."
- "We define a web application like any software application that depends on the web for proper implementation" (Gellersen and Gaedke, 1999, p. 61.).
- "It's more than just a website. It is a client-server using a web browser as the client program, application, and performs an interactive service connecting to servers on the Internet. A website simply displays static file content. A web application presents content dynamically adapted based on request parameters, tracking user behavior and security considerations" (Shklar and Rosen, 2003).
- "A web application is based and runs a web system to add business functionality. In simple terms, a web application is a web system that allows users to run business logic with a web browser" (Pearsonhighered, 2014, p. 9).

From these definitions, it abstracted that a web application is more than a website, presents information dynamically and operates in a web environment using as a primary means of web browsers. For this book work, the last two definitions were taken as they are more specific and complete.

The characteristics that web applications investigated in the literature (Borland Software Corporation, 2002; Finkelstein et al., 2004; Chong et al., 2007; Gellersen and Gaedke, 1999; Shklar and Rosen, 2003; Pearsonhighered, 2014) mainly relate to:

- **Client-Server Application:** "Network architecture where there is a relationship between processes requesting services (clients) and processes that respond to these services (server)" (Luján, 2002, p. 40).
- **Multi-Platform:** This indicates that the application can be used on any operating system (RAE, 2015).
- **Present Dynamic Information:** The content is displayed dynamically, i.e., based on application parameters, behavior tracking, and safety considerations.
- It requires a web browser client-side and a web server on the server-side.
- Web applications are available to anyone with internet access.

For the web application to be developed, the aforementioned characteristics are important because it allows to develop an application that can run on any operating system, use the client-server architecture allowing to a separation of the functions of both client-side and server, accessible from any web browser with internet access, allowing access to the application when needed and finally make use of information that is shown to the customer in a dynamic way.

CHAPTER 7

Thought, Creativity, and Machines

CONTENTS

Before discussing, the possibility that a machine thinks it is essential to agree on a definition of acceptable thought from a logical and empirical prism. Well, indeed, only if we clarify the most general and parsimonious concept of thinking we can get into the current debate about thinking machines.

The truth is that the important developments produced in research on artificial intelligence (AI) require foster a deeper dialogue between philosophy, science, and technology. In fact, we think we understand the nature and limits of human thought represents the great frontier of reason, because we inevitably raise the following questions: from electronic circuits, can we create awareness, a mind capable of abstracting up to realize their own existence? To what extent is the abstract thought an exclusive property of the human species? What's beyond ourselves, or perhaps we are the final season of evolution in its biological and cultural dimensions?

Ultimately, what is at stake is the meaning of "thinking" and, even more, the meaning of humanity.

Few notions seem as intuitively valid as that of "thinking." All think we know what it means. However, recognizing ignorance and try to remedy it is the preeminent way to the most genuine philosophical reflection. And just notice the meaning of "thinking" to easily notice the inadequacy of many of our concepts.

The main book will try to defend in this article is simple: if we give the ontological dualism (not necessarily the epistemological, or the property, but the ontological assumption that there are two kinds of reality: matter and spirit), not we see arguments against the possibility that machines running higher-order cognitive functions traditionally attributed exclusively to humans.

And our distinguished engineer and inventor Leonardo Torres foreshadowed the immense power of AI when he wrote:

We try to show in this note-from a purely theoretical view that it is always possible to construct an automaton whose actions, all depend on certain more or less numerous circumstances, obeying rules that may be imposed arbitrarily on the time of construction. Obviously, these rules must be such as sufficient to determine at any time, without any uncertainty, the behavior of the PLC. He thought no doubt that the automaton to respond reasonably, would need to make the same reasoning, whereas in this case, as in all others, the builder who would think about him beforehand. We believe we have shown, with all the foregoing, it can easily conceive for an automaton theoretical possibility to determine their action at a given moment, weighing all the circumstances to be taken into consideration for the work entrusted to him (Torres Quevedo, 2003, pp. 11–13).

No doubt, that Torres Quevedo showed deeply optimistic about the possibility of constructing a thinking machine. In the wake of many of the great pioneers of research in computer science, he believed that such unfathomable and philosophically broad as thought concept was fully susceptible to scientific enlightenment, capable of breaking the spell of impenetrability apparent and irreducible mysticism done by centuries of dualist approaches (tacit or explicit). Thus, the most genuine properties of the mind would be mechanically reproducible, thereby facilitating the emergence of a true AI.

It, therefore, seems imperative to clarify philosophically the basic notes of the act of thought as such, before addressing the question of the feasibility of an artificial thought.

However, it is also necessary to note that an excess of analytical rigor can lead us to exclude or neglect certain aspects of thought, for having too much pruning tree branches and placing ourselves toiled greatly to decompose without then recompose the puzzle.

Although the integration of knowledge (Blanco, 2018, p. 23ff) in the book have discussed the possible essential notes of thought in its most abstract and universal sense, for the sake of conceptual completeness we consider it appropriate to reiterate here the most important theses of this writing, later to attack the problem of thinking machines.

Loosely, thought can be defined as an association of mental content. This feature seems to be, in fact, the fundamental element of all kinds of thought, any biological species capable of being the subject of thought. Certainly, it would be necessary to refine this meaning. It should be noted, for example, which is a mental content and exactly how they are associated. In any case, it is incontestable that all forms of analysis and selection of options require prior association of mental contents. Thinking implies then ponders this content, monitor, discriminate according to some criterion. This relationship of ideas, however vague we please, be expressed in language, referred to as a system useful for those who can use signs. Thus, in the act of thinking, we are merely a set of relationships between mental contents through logical constants articulated in a specific language (which can be interpreted as an intelligible internal representation for a cognitive agent that produces and uses). In this manipulation of mental content, the agent uses symbolic expressions concerning actual or potential objects.

Thus, it can be said that thinking involves designing a monitoring system to oversee the content at issue in that particular thought. When thinking, the subject grips the elements constituting said contents assimilates a logical sequence by developing a function comprising its entirety. The design of this function can be interpreted as a process categorization, in which one of the possible configurations of the relationship between the elements of that mental association in order to follow a specific path is selected inferential.

From this perspective, you think will consist primarily of the ability to grasp and associate mental contents through a formal system in which it is possible to articulate (a "language"). Thus, the act of thinking would involve the creation and selection of correlations between mental content and a symbol. This relationship between mental content by logical constants allows anticipate result (a consequence, a logical inference may be correct, incorrect, or indeterminate). When thinking is then possible to develop a framework "meta" a virtual space wider than mental contents that integrate correlations own: a system of ideas. This system can be viewed as essentially equivalent to design a function that covers mental contents ("objects"), connected under a number of logical factors. Of course, these correlations can be univocal (if possible to design one correspondence between each mental content and a particular referent real or possible-) plurals or, if different objects may correspond to each mental content, or if different mental contents may correspond to each object. A more rigorous and meaningful thought objective tend to establish relationships between mental content and objects.

If the thought process aspires to be strictly rational, it must satisfy certain consistency rules and should be aware of its initial premises, in order to chart a logical path leading from them to conclusions. Rationality (which is, after all, one of the possible kinds of thinking) we interpret as well as the ability to organize information based on some premises and rules of inference. The most rational thinking is that with fewer assumptions get to integrate a greater amount of information. Therefore, rationality involves cognitive efficiency when a logical development base (here, logic refers to the process of inference as such, the way of thinking).

Synthetically, thinking we then presented as a link between mental contents through logical and grammatical constants. True to outline just stated, such a fact can also be interpreted as designing a function with an application domain: the objects on which that thought versa. However, this analysis of the fundamental characteristics of thought would be incomplete without distinguishing between the perspective of the rules and intuitions.

In its algorithmic or formal aspect, rational thinking is structured by rules guaranteeing the possibility to reach consistent conclusions, and the thinking subject must show proficiency in the use of these rules. However, this thought must be supervised by a person who assimilates the contents and displays capable of grasping a meaning, a unitary sense of all mental contents that make up that specific thought. This assimilation of the object as such (either a concept, a principle of the reason or the integration of both within a proposition), assessed as a unitary dimension and not only the individual elements constituting the object appears report a genuinely "intuitive" facet of the mind, where analytic decomposition of the parts that come into play in thought content gives the token to the development of a synthetic unit. It is not enough, therefore the blind following of syntactic rules: it is necessary to take care of them, even precariously.

These considerations do not imply, however, accept a kind of unilateral and despotic primacy of intuitive on the rational, as if in thought unobtainable comparable elements to a logical and scientific understanding. In fact, the contents of our intuitions are to be subsumed, in one way or another, in the general mechanisms of rational thought in the rules that guide our intellectual processes. It would not be an exaggeration to say that intuitions obey, indeed, internal rules, so the dream of conquering a purely explanatory understanding of human thought would not have to stand as a goal denied to our most solid scientific efforts.

In short, in every thought, it is possible to identify at least two kinds of objects: content ("mental images") and logical relationships (rules articulated around logical constants that establish relationships between these contents). When thinking we apply a set of logical categories to our representations of external and internal reality to our mind.

It certainly is a conceptual division, which does not have to involve a genuine temporary separation between the two processes, making mental representations and association of its contents.

7.1. THE ARTIFICIAL CREATIVITY

To think, to relate mental contents, the human mind is not limited to assimilate information, but also actively organized. We behold, thus some degree of creativity in this process of gestation of new ideas and new frameworks.

"The map is not the territory" because there is always an asymmetry between reality and its representation, which has to do with the creative organization of information through concepts and conceptual systems. Our minds made representations of reality that condenses into groups of symbols,

In fact, in the brief description of the act of thinking that we raised in the previous paragraphs, we have been forced to rely not on purely algorithmic elements (not subsumable i.e., in a program of well-defined instructions), but intuitive and, in a way, creative. However, they should not be considered creative as if they had led to the emergence of realities ex nihilo, the birth of a real novum, but in relation to the contents present; creative because there is a break, a leap that, in our opinion, is summarized very well in the notion of "analogy."

We should, therefore, consider the question of the nature of creativity.

We do not intend to summarize the important work of neuroscientific research have been carried out in recent years, but outlining some philosophical suggestions that can help us clarify this question so deep and inescapable, since it affects one of the most dazzling dimensions human mind: the ability to gestate the new.

Between idealizing a mystical vision and creativity and be a purely rationalist perspective, in our view, not eclectic, but integrative intermediate position. Unraveling the neurobiological processes underlying the genesis of a new idea is perfectly compatible with appreciate the philosophical value of the power that holds the human mind to create, i.e., to open new horizons for reflection, expand our conceptual frameworks and imagine unforeseen connections between the phenomena of the world and thought. In fact, we are convinced that only a deeper understanding of the precise brain mechanisms involved in this extraordinary ability allows us to discover how neurobiological processes and historical and cultural contexts that shape the various manifestations of human creativity are intertwined. It will also help us to properly interpret their expressions in other species, for although it seems undeniable that the expansion of the prefrontal cortices has immeasurably increased creative abilities of Homo sapiens. It is possible to discern unquestionable signs of creativity in many animals, whose understanding demands transcend rigid explanations in terms of reaction to stimuli and adaptation to environmental pressures to recognize genuine creative skills.

Indeed, it is this inevitable convergence of causalities "bottom-up" and "top-down" which highlights the failure of both a purely cerebral and neurophysiological understanding of creativity as a purely social study, based on extrinsic factors the structures and functions of the human mind itself. Moreover, research on the mechanisms regulating the plasticity of the human brain appears to calls to provide an increasingly strong link between bottom-up and top-down processes. These works do but to show that we are not certain to think of a concrete and irrevocably to possess this or that provision of synaptic connections, but with a relatively rigid genetic program instructions may modify neural connections in interaction with the environment, with the external, with the social and cultural environment in which sail (cf. Merzenich et al., 1988). This happy indeterminacy of the architecture of our neural connections emanates a remarkable degree of organizational flexibility, configurative wealth without which it would be impossible to explain how the mind learns and eventually create the new.

From a phenomenological point of view, in any creative act appearing elements of continuity and divergence. No creation breaks radically with the above, it is always possible to identify links with preceding logic elements and materials. Create implies, in a way, "remember," or at least find new connections between objects that were probably already familiar (cf. Benedek et al., 2014). However, it is clear that there is also a divergence from the above, a genuine innovation that even without cleavable suddenly from a logical route, not limited to evoke precursor ideas, but provides a new configuration of the objects mental.

In this kind of structured randomness, the creative mind constructs and reconstructs, innovates, and reorders, jumping into the vast space of possibilities of imagination. It does, however, preexisting material elements. Even the most picturesque creations of the imagination usually start (except very few exceptions) of known objects already accumulated experiences, reflections, and outlined. Well, indeed, with linear routes, sequential logic paths perfectly capable of elucidating that allow transition from an antecedent to consequent, in the creative process, is inevitable to distinguish a certain "break the logic symmetry," a series of conceptual leaps and figural which refer to the notion of "analogy" as no necessary relationship, though legitimate, between different by identifying common denominators. It is precisely in the development of homologies, or analog similarities between different elements, where lies one of the most productive tools of creativity. These homologies may be direct, if the connection between antecedent and consequent obvious or indirect, if the link is more remote.

In any case, the deeper logical and philosophical problem concerns not so much the ability to find unusual combinations of certain elements (an interesting analogy with the mechanism of variation/selection driving the evolution of species), but the possibility of the occurrence of a genuine Hiatal hatching a real novum within the human mind. In other words, beyond the concurrence of rational, emotional, spontaneous, or deliberate factors, what are the neurobiological causes of creative disruption? We hardly think that no microscopic continuity and even cognitive neurobiological level; the creative process would rather interpret a reorganization of mental contents comparable to phase transitions studying physics, which does not have to happen a complete and sharp break between antecedents and consequences, but a reconfiguration of the elements present.

It is, however, indirect homologies in the unlikely proposition or unsuspected connections, where we can admire one of the most beautiful, and mysterious ways of the great intellectual and artistic creations of mankind sources. Why did Newton the idea that there was a reasonable connection between the force that holds together the Earth and the Moon and that drops the apple tree is one of the most beautiful mysteries of the human mind. Is it something inexplicable, a supernatural miracle? We do not think so, as unlikely as they pleased this link between superlunary and sublunary Newton's contemporaries' legitimacy to seek a conceptual link between the two worlds was irreproachable, although contradicted centuries of reflection philosophical, scientific, and theological. It was, in fact, expected that sooner or later happen to any of his contemporaries, like Leibniz discovered calculus almost simultaneously Newton, or Wallace natural selection while Darwin, or Poincaré many of the principles of special relativity regardless of Einstein. We cannot forget, however, that the analysis of this issue seems inexorable appeal to the unique characteristics of the great minds of history intellectual, daughters of his time, certainly, but possessing some outstanding cognitive skills that allowed them to see and justify deeper and transcendental relationships between seemingly unrelated phenomena.

In the analogy, we can then discern a powerful heuristic principle, a facilitator of the genesis of new ideas, creativity in its most pure, and genuine sense instrument. The analogy lacks the probative value of logical inference, but exhibits an immense inspiring potential to explore new connections between phenomena and new approaches to existing problems. It stands as a general structure of imagination that allows us to find homologies between objects and concepts whose properties keep some relationship, however weak and remote it may seem. Sheltered in understanding the similarities between the formation and properties of certain objects and categories, enables us to venture on new scenarios and transcend the rigid requirements of strict logical inference. Resplendence therefore mainly as a construction process which is not limited to display the contents of the premises, but dares to propose innovative elements beyond the expected results of a logical connection. Moreover, in some cases that creation is channeled through the destruction of previous forms and their replacement by others.

Almost inexorably in all bold and potentially disruptive analogy shines the light of intuition, an intense and hardly transferable subjective perception that is imbued with a fruitful uncertainty; outside the canons of rigorous and unequivocally valid rational demonstration, but endowed with a boundless creative force. How and why these intuitions occur? Why only bless some minds? They are the logical consequence of training, familiarity with a particular domain of knowledge and action? A computer would support that logic uncertainty surrounding human intuition, creativity window?

In fact, creativity only seems to excel in its entire splendor where no possibility of ambiguity, vagueness, and incompleteness; where it is questionable fundamentals, developments, and consequences. Logical reasoning is well formulated apodictically necessary. In him there glimpses of creative freedom. However, it is necessary to create cross the barriers of the particular logical necessity and expand the horizon of reflection, to identify new evidence and new connections. Great thoughts assume the paradox and resolved in a new framework, a sort of recapitulation of Aufhebung. We contemplate in Einstein, who reconciled Newtonian mechanics with Maxwell's electromagnetism realizing that they were compatible within a broader and deeper physical model.

7.2. MACHINES AND CONSCIOUSNESS

Can he intone a machine think consciously, i.e., relate contents and refer to herself, to the perception of their own identity? Can he reason order thoughts? Will you learn to tolerate uncertainty and ambiguity, vestibules of creativity?

An easy answer will argue that everything depends on how we define the concept of "conscious thought" (if this binomial is not tautological). However, it seems clear that if we establish a too demanding idea of consciousness, how can we know that we, human beings, have in reality rather than just run purely mechanical and automated actions, thoughtless fruits of an alien algorithmic process a hypothetical and inscrutable me? How do you know that consciousness is owned by someone other than the conscious subject that perceives such a vivid, intimate, and almost incommunicable way, as a concomitant feature their own cognitive acts?

Therefore, it is essential to agree on a working definition of consciousness, to be reconcilable with the thought for minimally elucidate the idea of "conscious thought," that is, of that kind of thinking that the subject can take over. Well, in fact, the discussion on the concept of thought that we outlined in the first section is easy to deduce that, in our opinion, in its deepest sense it is revealed as an antithetical phenomenon unconscious, or a mere concatenation stimuli and responses on which the thinking subject would have no control. From this philosophical perspective, thinking necessarily involves a subject to monitor the process of association of ideas, to appropriate it.

So, the first approach consisted of a mere association of ideas shown after further analysis, as an apprehension of those connections between mental contents, an act involving a subjective monitoring beyond a chain of images. Even vaguely, this notion points to the problem of consciousness and how it relates to thought.

We recognize that beats here the profound and inescapable difficulties of self-consciousness, the Kantian transcendental apperception, action that transcends priori all possible contents: self-reflection. Despite the seriousness of the question, la question is whether this subjective instance conceivable in organic continuity with the most basic brain structures and less complex biological forms, in which case the dualistic book postulates an ontological split between the material and mental subjectivity substrate, lose effectiveness. It would then not be illusory to strive to build an artificial consciousness thinking machines, as reasonably would know the structure and properties of such an elusive phenomenon. It seems clear, though, that if consciousness has arisen in an evolutionary manner (as teaches us the application of the theory of evolution to the development of the mental faculties of Homo sapiens), there must be a biological mechanism underlying scientific explanation of how they appeared phylogenetically our cognitive skills. Of course, this question could also reproduce the ontogenetic scale.

As we face one of the most profound and fascinating philosophical and neuroscientific research mysteries, we will discuss only some basic ideas that can illuminate fundamental aspects of this question, as pressing as inveterate. Advances in understanding the neurobiological mechanisms of consciousness have been remarkable. Although important aspects remain today covered with a thick veil of mystery, we find no reason to believe that these enigmas have to last forever, "ignoramus, non-ignorabimus thirst." In fact, at least from Baars (1988a, 2005) and, more recently, Dehaene, and Changeux (cf. Dehaene et al., 2006, 2017) have proposed theoretical models susceptible contrast experimental. Intended to validate or refute hypotheses about the nature of consciousness, many of these experimental tests relate, for example, on the relationship between the unconscious and the conscious perception (binocular rivalry, masked stimuli, competition between images.).[1].

Simplified way, consciousness can be seen as a system of monitoring information processed by the brain. It's no wonder, in fact, that evolution has led to the birth of such a cognitive system. Its objective would not be other than to filter and control information as heterogeneous as that constantly bombards our senses.

It can be argued, however, that this conception of consciousness as a monitoring system, as an extra element that adds a new dimension to the analysis of available information (an external body), sins of great ingenuity, it does not justify the real need of consciousness. Indeed, it could be argued that the monitoring device would work perfectly but lacked awareness and was a mere zombie. However, it seems reasonable to think that consciousness adds an undeniable evolutionary advantage, not included in the purely mechanical monitoring and unaware of the information treated by the subject. In our opinion, the prospect of the first person incorporates a split between subject and object offering great and profound benefits that are able to apply: confers a greater degree of independence from the environment, and even about our own mental states, it comes to "judge" from outside. What is your ultimate mechanism? Is it enough to invoke a duality between perception and association, made possible by the neuroanatomical organization of the human brain in different areas, a charge of perceiving and associating other information perceived? We think so, at least from a conceptual point of view. However, it is undeniable that much still remains to fully clarify the specific neurobiological and cognitive processes, if such an ambitious goal can ever be completed, which would culminate one of the most exciting intellectual pursuits undertaken by the human species:

The truth is that the mind is, above all, a unifying force, perceptions generating unit. Even invaded by heterogeneous information, it is able to select some items and discarding others. This operation is already a hint

1

of conscience, interpreted as a control or monitoring information available. Consciousness is presented as a kind of filter, suitable for selectively attend to some content and exclude others. The higher and more complex consciousness implies, however, that selected refer to oneself, to a subjective instance, an elusive me information. Is the act of "knowing that one knows" the possibility that the subject knows he knows. Of course, this insight is one of the most intricate aspects when addressing the nature of consciousness[2].

Is it plausible that a computer reaches this enigmatic self-referentiality, so deep in possession of the information level, self-awareness?

Logically, if we consider that the machines are limited to obey instruction programs previously designed by humans, to receive inputs that by inference rules generate outputs, it is difficult that we give them the ability to think creatively as humans. These machines would be mere automatons; rigid executors of assignments that process information, but not assimilate, not ponderarían, not a subjective instance would refer to an individual consciousness. Deprived of the ability to establish a clear boundary between the stimulus (input and system design, which are given by the human mind) and the response (the inexorable behavior of a machine under design rules), it seems inconceivable attributed to a machine the ability to consciously reflect,

However, this conception of machines does not have to exhaust all possible models for designing an AI. In the creation of more advanced machines, which are not limited to learn a program instruction, but they learn themselves to learn and get to develop their own instructions, lies one of the most prolific technological innovations of recent decades[3].

In addition, computational engineering learning can benefit greatly from our understanding of biological phenomena, the fruitful intertwining of variation and selection that defines evolutionary processes, instruction

2. Despite this difficulty, can be designed precise experiments that measure levels reportability (cf. Dehaeneetalii, 2017). It is also clear that sometimes we are aware and some not, then there must be a function of continuity between the two states, although it virtually imperceptible change. Consciousness, therefore, would not necessarily be seen as a process of "all or nothing" but consciousness scales exist. However, it is also likely to be some sort of critical threshold, a notion that would not present major problems for science, used in many branches of knowledge to the idea of critical points and ruptures of symmetry.

3 For an overview of the so-called machine learning, cf. Alpaydin, 2009; on unsupervised learning, cf. Hastie Etalii, 2009.

programs which are elastic and flexible to the environment. Torres Quevedo and realized it, because "it is necessary that automata imitate living things, executing their actions under the impressions they receive with and adapting their behavior to the circumstances" (Torres, 2003, p. 10). Such an ability to learn to learn positive reinforcement encourages a greater degree of adaptability to a changing environment, a diaphanous skill gradually when the initial screening inferences and subject to the luminous contrast of external factors. It is precisely here,

It would, however, extremely naive to think that reproduce the essential elements of biological phenomena computational scale is easy. In fact, the study of biological processes seems inevitable appeal to the existence of a design unit; an organic character overcomes the diversity of members and gives the whole articulation, consistency, and a high degree of unification between the parts. The living (especially those with a more evolved nervous system) acts as a whole, it exercises control over parts and objectives proposed. How to imitate this extraordinary teleology, this intriguing self-configuration capability treasured living beings, represents one of the most profound challenges for AI, because in it the real qualitative leap between automatism and spontaneity resides. It is not naive, though, believe that the visions overly idealized animal subjectivity (the including human), ready to enthrone in an arcane metaphysical seat where reign as conjectured edge of the world, are likely to be dissolved by concepts that inspired neuroscience, evolutionary biology and the study of the natural history of life on Earth, show how gradually may have arisen that ability to self-perception that stands as one of the greatest enigmas of science.

Therefore, designing similar machines to living organisms, able not only to process information, but also to become aware of their own existence and to equip themselves with purposes of self-determination (and even self-destruct), it does not have to establish itself a utopian goal. But it will need to learn more about the "intelligence" (biological) that what "artificial" fully understand what are the most distinctive features of animal intelligence are and understand their biological roots to imitate or reliably overcome this skill so remarkable that crown its peak in the human species.

We see, in short, an intrinsic inability to reproduce simple computations and complex processes that occur in the brain. Separate issue is the size of a project that would involve condensing and even transcend technologically millions of years of biological evolution, combinations of genetic variations, natural, and learning selection transmitted through culture, where the method of trial and error had to play a fundamental role. However, this difficulty does not have to be absolute, because even today we do not know the limits of wit, imagination, and creativity of human beings to solve problems and, even more, to invent new ones and expand the radius possible.

7.3. APPLICATIONS OF ARTIFICIAL INTELLIGENCE (AI) IN EVERYDAY LIFE

AI today is applied to hundreds of different fields, from mobile phone applications to rural areas to monitor crops and livestock. But the most common and known uses for people are called recommendation systems, such as those found in Spotify, Netflix, Amazon, among others. Where we offer suggestions based on series/movies we've previewed or music, we tend to listen. This allows us to focus on other tasks, we need not waste time looking for something new, or sorting our mail, it is normal and it does a computer and that's all about. People now have more time than ever. They are able to pursue their passions through the use of technology and mass communication and are able to do many more things that seemed impossible a few decades ago. There are others who say that to be doing so many things cannot afford the time. But clearly, this means we are making a greater number of tasks in the same period compared to previous years. "Machine learning is already incorporated into our lives. It is incorporating tasks already seem insignificant because the mail is ordered only and also automates simple tasks that we do not take much time to think, how to turn on a light or jot down a reminder. "-JD De Gourville how to turn on a light or jot down a reminder. "

People are living a breakthrough. It is increasingly common to talk to a program, either on our phone or computer when we need help with a product or service or with less meaningful tasks like turning on a light when we get home. "It is used much automating simple tasks and is something that for many people is already common" (J. Gourville). This is being made possible by a more capable and demanding society, as well as cheaper technology. Today, computers are far more powerful than they used to be and allow people to invent innovative products and services to the world are really a nicer place. Ambos respondents agree with the fact that the AI will shape the future tremendously, giving people more opportunities like never before had. Bloomberg said that "the AI will add $15.7 billion to the global economy by 2030." In the last 5 years, we have seen how this fact is coming true in our day-to-day. While this may seem an optimistic view, there are some people who believe that AI will take us to a world like terminator, where the machines will try to kill humanity. Respondents do not see this scenario as a possible outcome. "These systems are designed to help a person and used as a tool, not to become a threat" (J. M. Corchado). In fact, we are still far from building something like this, and this technology has to mature more to replace those in the "human tasks."

7.4. AI AND SOCIETY

The AI will help emerging transcend more developed countries, if this is one of the goals of nations. As mentioned above, the AI will inject hundreds of millions of dollars to the global economy, and if emerging countries invest in research, it can be placed on top and open many doors for future better. But, did most vulnerable parties will benefit of society with the use of AI? Probably nothing will change. One respondent said he believes that the AI generates a wider gap in society, but neither reduced. "we think it's an opportunity to get closer to more developed countries, but the truth is it will end up generating more than a gap" (J. Grouville).

We must understand that even though this technology will improve all of our lives, not help eradicate poverty or create any major structural change in society.

7.5. IMPACTS OF USING MACHINES TO PERFORM HUMAN TASKS

The main social impact of AI is replacing workers with machines, either in the productive process industries 4.0 or at the tip of the chain, such as customer service. All these activities have already begun testing robots, some showing performance quite satisfactory results. This does not mean that humans will be completely replaced, but will be seen as liberation from the most physically intensive and less desired tasks. AI does not have to be seen as a replacement for us, but as a tool. -G. Kasparov.

AI is a tool to make people work more efficient and easier. With regard to the work, it is true that some will disappear, but those are jobs that require repetitive tasks with few skills, as the driver, cashier or working in a call center. "And we do not think anyone has the vocation to be cash" (J. Grouville). The disappearance of these jobs allows people explore their tastes and develop skills in the future will be better paid or can actually do for pleasure instead of having another alternative. On the other hand, there will be new jobs, for example in the area of maintenance of these machines or, for example, for the development of these, although it is true that the same number of researchers do not require car drivers. But that's far in the future this may change and may be reversed.

Future researchers could rely on to make AI applications easier to use, produce, and adopt worldwide, as they will benefit emerging countries to add millions of dollars to its economy. It truly is the future and no one should be left behind. This will help researchers to have a great computational power to use in any project they want, as the diagnosis of diseases that tend to go unnoticed, or analyze large amounts of data and then display statistics in a very short time.

7.6. CHANGES GENERATED BY ARTIFICIAL INTELLIGENCE (AI) IN THE WAY PEOPLE MAKE

As we mentioned earlier, AI and he is giving a new shape to our lives. Technologies that easily incorporate into our lives without even realizing it, such as using recommendation systems or Google himself. Soon they influence our behaviors, whether for good or ill. One of the changes mentioned by respondents, J. Gourville, is that AI has impacted on our way to view tasks. By this, he means that today we think differently in terms of the complexity of a certain task we have to perform, thanks to the tools we have to provide us with information or even do it for us, like turn on a light or make an order a virtual assistant. Now we see small tasks like things we do not want to do because in our head we are automated, for example, search for information in a book now we can download the book and directly find what we're looking for, use the alarm clock phone, organize files and documents, etc. Years ago, nobody would have imagined that we could ask our phone to locate a historic date for us or we can spend the playlist we were listening recently. But today is not unusual, it is very common. We are saving time and energy to use it on other tasks. We should no longer visit the city to look for specialists of certain tasks when we have a phone that is a specialist in everything.

Closing the subject of interviews, it can be concluded that both respondents agree that AI and took center stage in our lives, and that this was introduced in a subtle way, unannounced massively. Thus generating a gradual change in our way of doing certain tasks. As already mentioned, if we ask our parents about certain tasks and compare their answers with ours, we can see big differences. These technologies are adopted globally and giving a new shape to our lives, helping us to be more productive and efficient in our daily lives, and slowly eliminating those jobs that do not help us to improve personally, giving us the space to explore new interests.

In this section, we will present the results of a survey of 70 people, where people interviewed were between 14 and 23 years. In this, we asked about general topics of AI with focus on normally we consume every day, to see how aware the common user is. We also obtained information about some of their behaviors regarding the use of machine learning technologies and their thoughts about them.

The following chart can be seen as 57% of respondents are male, while 42% are women. It may be that the issue has seemed more interesting to men them, because it is linked to careers and preferences in which statistically more men than women are. In addition to gender, 57% are people between 15 and 18 years while 30% are between 19 and 23 only 12% are over 24 we found a relationship in which people the range of 18 to 24, more familiar with the subject, because of their answers and their explanations of certain questions that were discussed later.

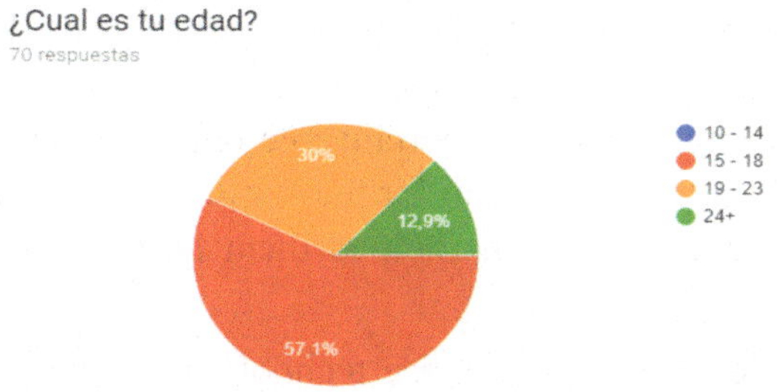

As we can see in the charts below most respondents possess great knowledge of electronics, such as smartphones and computer devices, as marked as dominated and feel comfortable using. Besides their daily hours of use, they are quite high, with 46% between 2 and 4 hours, 40% between 5 and 7 hours and 14% over 7 hours. This is because as we spoke previously, technology is already part of our lives and almost all use to work with our electronic devices and the Internet.

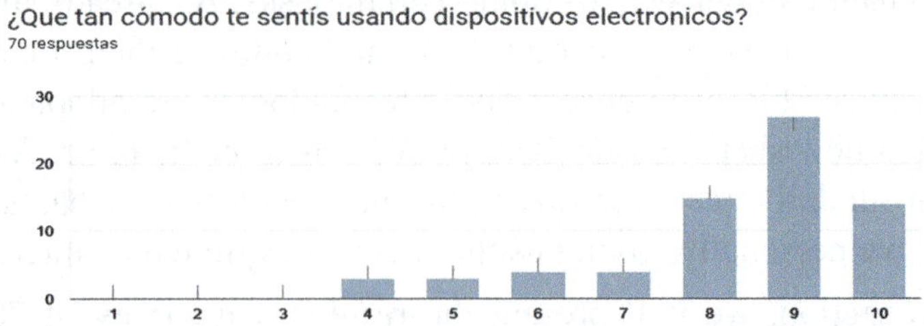

As we move more in the survey, we found that 47% of respondents recognize use applications that apply AI or machine learning. While 47%, do not know. This is important to note, because all applications use these technologies, from Google to Spotify or Netflix. But only 58% say they recognize. This comes from the idea that Machine Learning and AI are not commonly spoken in our day-to-day, but the truth is they are present. They are also not new, since Google already has more than 15 years using these algorithms, Netflix Spotify 5. Clearly, 10 and these applications and algorithms are becoming increasingly recognized due to the impact they are generating.

Interestingly only 47% recognized the term AI in the previous question, but 96% confirmed using or ever used these applications in the form of suggestions from videos or virtual assistants like Siri. This clarifies that not everyone is aware of what this technology even use it. This does not mean that this evil, as many people drive without knowing how a car works or use a microwave without knowing what this really does to our food. Anyway, clearly, the machine learning plays an important role in the lives of people, generating small conveniences are grateful for the common user, since 83% of them said they use these suggestions helped them find new channels/ artists.

Recent growth and development of these technologies generated 86% of respondents believe that handles different times compared to its previous generation, their parents. Whether for a few things, many people feel that 58% of these technologies make them work and be more productive, so they are more efficient when searching for information or work, while 38% think they lose long compared to their parents. This can come from the hand of applications like Instagram or other social networks using machine learning to spend more time in them, suggesting we're not content to subscribed, but can now simultaneously LIKE introduce ads based on our interests.

Finally, as the last question, we wanted to know whether the use of the aforementioned or other applications that use AI or machine learning had generated a change in the behavior of respondents. To which 55% said yes. The most common response they feel they have more time, and that can perform tasks more quickly and efficiently, as have their paid automatically home banking sites or accounts. Besides some responded that their behaviors were affected by having their musical tastes suggestions were expanded and came out of always hearing the same artists to meet new ones.

After analyzing the surveys, a better understanding of the situation with regard to the common user had. It was understood that the term AI is well known with results of 47.1% and over 90% of respondents claimed to have used some of its applications. We can clearly see on the charts and in the comments on the last question, respondents acknowledge that perform certain tasks in a different way. So as the hypothesis says, AI has changed the way people do. Among the answers, we can find some like everything is faster; things look easier and save time.

At the end of my research, resume my specific objectives:

- Investigate the use and applications of AI in everyday life.
- Explain the changes that AI-generated in the way of thinking and making people.
- Explain the impacts of using machines to perform human tasks.

In which it was understood that AI has many applications in our daily lives, for more complex tasks such as monitoring the amount of water in plantations in the field until we can turn on a light with the use of voice. It was understood changes in the way people do, so that we are able to face problems with a friendlier look by using tools that help us work such as Google. Also was assumed that therefore, this technology is developed, it will always be a tool for man, and not a replacement. This means that not all jobs will disappear, and if they will be for the greater good. Resulting in new jobs in other areas, such as the development and maintenance of these technologies.

In conclusion, AI has come a long way since his first appearances in the mid-1950s, and it is growing at a rapid pace. We can easily see how important it is to our daily lives and the impact it has created in ourselves. People have changed. People now perform tasks in a different way than they used to. How to forget tasks performed alone, such as paying certain bills. They assume things that in the past required work, time, and effort. And no longer imagine life without these little details that really make it easier. Machine learning and AI are making our lives are different, easier. They are giving people what they want when they want it. The concept of time has changed and became more valuable now. Everyone should be doing something all the time, and the AI has more liberal. It will shape the future for the better; we can draw from our minds the vision of the apocalyptic future full of terminators, and begin to see the world and the advancement of this technology as a breaking point where from now, the world becomes a better place. There are people who know and are creating a change in their lives and the lives of others in the form of businesses and projects such as those mentioned above. They begin to see the world and the advancement of this technology as a breaking point where from now, the world becomes a better place. There are people who know and are creating a change in their lives and the lives of others in the form of businesses and projects such as those mentioned above.

Regarding my hypothesis "AI and its branches have helped and help people automate everyday and work tasks because of its potential which is able to replace work done by humans that generates a change in the way to do the things." We came to the conclusion that AI has created a change in the way we do, quickly oriented, automation, and efficiency. So that people have become accustomed to certain comforts that did not have before and today are made possible by technology, and more specifically to advances in AI. Tasks like having categorized mail, applications like YouTube or Netflix series or recommend us based on what we like video, or think that we like.

On the other hand, since the advent of AI and more specifically Google, people were flooded with knowledge at their fingertips, resulting in companies not stop learning new songs, and thanks to AI discovered new areas of interest in which to investigate and invest time. In a way, the forms were affected to people, but as we do not think they are investigated, the extent to which we imagined before starting the investigation.

After researching and analyzing surveys and interviews, we came to the conclusion that as my hypothesis, use, and adoption of AI and machine learning says it has generated a change in the way people do. So my hypothesis is correct.

Although it is noteworthy that for more than that if a change is generated in the way of making people, this was not as significant as thought before starting my research. They feel they have more time, more likely to perform tasks that interest them easier to find certain products, artists, and even people. AI, slowly but progressively it introduced changes that began to reshape our behavior and thoughts, opening ourselves to greater opportunities when performing almost any task.

AI, besides its branch, which is the most impact machine learning. Very palpable impact for nearly 20 years. 20 years ago, it is usual that there are machine learning applications that impact our lives. The closest to us is what we call recommender systems such as YouTube, Amazon, or Google.

When we walk in and through our consumption history, or because we're watching a product machine learning algorithms are applied.

AI in that environment all have very habituated. It's all custom. The mail also with spam filters or folders in which we classify mails. Much work selection and curing of the information. Machine learning is the AI applied. Machine learning is a better-defined concept.

Specifically, an application is said to be a learning machine that does improve their performance on a task as it processes information. As we learn, it gets better. Differently traditionally having to modify the code.

The idea is that as we have more information, application performance improves automatically.

Other pioneers were the banking and insurance industries. Analyzing risks and transaction data for finding patterns. When credit cards are copied, patterns can be detected and alert system.

Machine learning algorithms look for patterns. They are classifiers; they put a label on something. If a transaction is fraudulent or not, if someone is likely to buy something or not. Recognize objects using computer vision, and for autonomous cars that put the labels to the environment.

AI is vast and varied, but machine learning is already incorporated into our lives. It is incorporating tasks as seemingly insignificant as the mail is ordered alone, and automating simple tasks that we do not take a long time to think about them, like turning a light or score a reminder.

We will use much automating simple tasks. Another will be the use of bots in call centers that is something that already comes. Virtual assistants not only as Alexa or Google assistant, but also bots on customer service Facebook or anywhere. Eliminate the menus on pages so that we attend word to make a table. There will be an important part of the customer service impact. We understand that the bots talking to we normally do not have to give them precise instructions. Online support improvements that will be implemented massively. Should improve customer service by not having to wait for an operator. They could end generalities as presets a call. And they could deal with individual queries.

Many people see it as a threat. But the jobs are repetitive pointing or no one wants to do. We do not think anyone has the vocation to work in a call center. A phrase that Kasparov said: "AI not has to look like someone who is going to replace, but as someone who is going to promote it will be a support tool." By eliminating tedious work, AI can be applied to legal and illegal activities; it can be applied to hacking and pass security barriers.

In general, the major technological advances have been used for good and for evil. Generally, they end up having positive impacts, but the crimes and the military will be enforced by the use of AI. But it will use the two sides, a kind of chess game. AIs will be possible to see the two sides.

It is calling for projects to be canceled, but we know that's not going to happen. But as for the labor impact, this is something that we ask a lot. People think that in three years it will be left without work. We have seen software that supposedly works better than an attorney to detect problems with contracts, or applications that can analyze and diagnose better than a doctor. But it should be viewed as a support tool and no replacement. Because if we're not prune doctor we have an application that is better than we to diagnose?

The machine learning is good for activities that require little time and depth of analysis. If there is a task that a person can do in one second or less, surely that task can be automated. They have to take into account the country's needs, economic capabilities, corruption, vision having its leaders. Here in Argentina, it is on the one hand private initiative that moves the market. This is commercial, system recommendations more to that side, odds safe. There was an Argentine who wanted to implement autonomous cars but ended up going to use it.

On the other hand, in the governmental area used in the AFIP more than anything, for information crosses the tax collection level. It is recommended that research in the area of health, because it is a very good tool to democratize access to health. AI applications because they serve us to diagnose, use is immediately scalable. It is an important opportunity. But the government does not give the ball and end up making a private company and will charge the government to implement it.

We think it's an opportunity to get closer to more developed countries, but the truth is it will end up generating more than a gap. AI does not always have a clear return. For developing countries, find it difficult to bend to this wave in the same way as developed countries. More a matter of vision that as a matter of resources. We are not seeing AI applications that apply to the upper sectors. At least at the level of consumption. Of course, there are exceptions, such as Tesla or some specialized services. We can see a gap in the future when there are services that are superior to people and charged expensive.

For now, we do not see an AI for the rich and another for the poor. If there is a collateral problem called algorithmic bias. This happens with data collection and training. As it may when evaluating résumés of our equipment and this could predict and review the criminal records of people and predict whether they are the best choice for a company.

In such a case, it may not come from lower sectors where a person is hired, because it shares traits with people who are nor were criminals.

AI is the way to solve complex problems efficiently. If the systems are well made allow real-time decisions and act against future events that can predict such a simple definition that only an expert of its size is able to give. Then, yes, everything is complicated. The challenges of all kinds, the thousands of branches encompassing discipline or the various professional profiles required.

One of the factors that most influence is that this is so is a more capable and demanding society, with problems more demanding, and cheaper technology. AI has until recently been expensive and their results were not immediate, reason was that needed a lot of data and much computation time due to the complexity of the calculations; Today, thanks to the abundance of information, supercomputers, and distributed computing power, we can get results faster and at a much lower cost, facilitating research in this field.

Regarding the warnings about the danger to the world, as Bill Gates spoke, Elon Musk or Stephen Hawking, we do not think pass. These systems are designed to be helpful to the human being, not to pose a threat and also, we are still far from building something like the human brain. Today the danger of autonomous computers is not real. In addition, it is now an emerging theme of ethics, where each program should be reviewed applying ethics of good and evil to avoid these problems with large numbers of users, and is calling them "social machines." Which they are computer systems whose behavior is fueled by a lot of users and which in turn have a great ability to influence them.

He also stressed the conceptual leap that involves designing intelligent systems (IS) capable of continuous learning and evolving with the problem, and the disruptive leap that has led -having the limitations of neural networks- introduce sociological elements of interaction algorithms to evolve randomly as nature does. Systems for analyzing feelings, opinions, and online reputation. That seems to be very interesting, and that is being carried out thanks to computer vision and natural language processing and written to understand that people want to convey. Other interesting projects are related to smart cities. A few months ago, we returned from Singapore, which solved the problem of shortage of physical space for storing surface, making it underground. An intelligent city is not one equipped with millions of sensors but which is very critical to the needs of citizens, inclusive, and respectful of the environment, causing the above redound into tangible benefits and demonstrable savings for citizens.

Another area that is beginning to see, if not in Latin America but in Europe and the United States if it is biotechnology and e-health. There is a project on monitoring brain activity to create a map of signals with different stimuli. Thus, through a sensitized helmet that communicates via Bluetooth with a wheelchair, the thought of something positive can be enough to move it. Robots for personal care in an aging population such as ours will also become highly relevant in the future and there are very interesting systems and specially designed to facilitate human-machine collaboration where they learn as they change the needs of patients.

Companies working with AI, mainly by selling data to large companies such as Google, will have a very high increase in turnover. We are talking about thousands of millions of dollars. They are not going to invest in the most vulnerable sectors. What we think is that maybe not everyone has access to AI in the same way. For example, hospitals in less developed countries may not have predictive technologies and diagnoses of diseases such as the near future may already have in Singapore. In these cases, if we can see a difference, but it's based on the country and its capabilities. On the other hand, a country like China, which invests heavily in the development of AI, it is possible that people can access more equitably to use because it is a program. No modern infrastructure for all our applications is required, just enough to develop the program and try to expand it as quickly and efficiently as possible. Good to be closing think now that AI is gaining headlines in scientific and computer items added to the increase in investments, will generate rapid development against what was proposed many years ago that never got to watch. Now we are closer and have more computational power, to be able to make applications that we see on television as a black mirror, and we think well times innovation for this sector come.

CHAPTER 8

The Future of AI Technology

CONTENTS

AI is one of the most fascinating areas but with more challenges in computer science and technology. This arose from the need of man to imitate his surrounding nature to the degree of imitation itself by systems or machines able to replace him in certain jobs or activities.

That is why AI programs promise to be the future of technology where today's machines or robots may join them recognition technologies voice and video.

Although we are far from a powerful computer system intelligence level and the cognitive human brain consists of about 100,000 million neurons always have the fear that if we reach this level this artificial intelligence (AI) could understand his now independent yet the human race and want to be at the same level. Although these sound like science fiction with the rapid advancement of technology this could leave just be in our imagination.

For now, should make good use of this advancing technology field for better development of systems that can help us better our standard of living such as medical expert systems that help us diagnose diseases and possible treatments, also intelligent systems (IS) help us in the field of mechanical engineering and the development of increasingly accurate and better machines to replace us in dangerous tasks such as the bomb, manufacturing with highly toxic chemicals or hazardous materials.

8.1. THE FUTURE IN THE AREA OF HEALTH

AI is a very wide range of studies, and constantly changing. However, the final product is always software. These programs, work product AI, are called intelligent systems (IS).

A IS incorporates knowledge drawn from the experience and expertise of human experts. Fields of application of such IS's are varied; think for example in a medical diagnostic system, or an integrated aid business decision-making system. In any case, an IS leaves some data and become information (knowledge), so that helps to make a decision. To convert data into useful information, we will use algorithms reasoning, learning, evolution, etc. In addition, the IS will always act in real-time, an increase in productivity.

For medical applications of AI, they are so broad that we cannot even summarize them all, so we will mention some of the most widely been used and some of the most common being used in present.

Two researchers from Indiana University have developed a model of AI that says they can identify and significantly better treatments offered by doctors to patients. Like the Watson computer, ready to help in cancer treatment, it is further evidence of how the management of large volumes of data in computers will have a profound impact on health systems.

The researchers have, it would be predictive modeling techniques that can get to make more accurate treatment decisions. Statistics affirm, with tests showed a 50% reduction in costs assumed in medicine and more than 40% improvement in terms of patient outcomes.

The idea behind the research Cassey Bennet and Kris Hauser is simple. If doctors can consider what is really happening from the beginning, rather than relying on intuition, better decisions would be taken.

The researchers worked with clinical, demographic data and other information on more than 6,700 patients who had diagnoses of clinical depression more severe, of which approximately 65% had chronic physical disorders such as diabetes, hypertension, or cardiovascular disease.

AI built a model using the so-called Markov Decision Process (which predicts the likelihood of future events based on the immediately preceding them) and considering the specific characteristics of these events in order to determine the odds. Essentially, the model considers the details of the current state of a patient and then determines the best action to make the best possible outcome.

Both researchers found through a simulation of 500 cases random model reduced the economic cost improvement of 58.5%. They found that the original model improved patient outcomes by almost 35%, and adjusting some parameters could reduce this figure to 41.9%.

Results that are in addition to the news coming from IBM and indicates that computers and managing and analyzing large volumes of data will be of great benefit in the future for health care.

For IBM, the company has announced two new commercial versions of Watson, one specifically designed to determine the best treatment for patients with lung cancer. It does this through the analysis of a "library" of millions of clinical data and medical research.

News that does not indicate that in the future is to replace the figure of doctors by an advanced AI; on the contrary, technology will complement the work of professionals, digesting large amounts of information on cases and investigations at a time record for the doctor to find the best possible treatment in each situation.

1. Artificial Heart: The first artificial heart implant occurred in 1982, and since then has evolved greatly in the matter. But keep in mind that the complexity facing their development remains still experimental material.

The most advanced model known is the AvioCor; this artificial heart has been shown to be effective for periods of time exceeding 500 days. All components are implanted inside the body and maintain minimal maintenance.

The implant respects the bloodstream, through connections with the main veins and arteries without internal sutures to prevent blood flow unimpeded. Artificial heart implantation requires, if a major surgery.

The artificial heart occupies the cavity leaving the heart after the patient was removed during surgery.

The material from which the artificial heart is built is a titanium alloy and, nonstick blood lightweight plastic.

How does it work? The key is that the artificial heart has flexible walls containing a silicone fluid. Inside thereof, an engine produces centrifugal force in the fluid, and therefore, in the flexible walls of the compartment. This control pressure (through the valve) is the main function of the operation of the artificial organ.

2. Artificial Retina: Japanese scientists have developed a system of artificial vision for the blind or people with an impaired sight which makes getting visual signals to the brain, reports The Inquirer magazine.

The manufacturer of ophthalmic products in Japan, Nidek, Professor YasuoTano, of Osaka University and Professor Jun Ota Nara Institute of Science and Technology worked together in the development of this system, which is composed of a sunglasses have built-in cameras filming some images of what lies in front of the subject and an electronic device that converts these images into digital signals.

In addition, the system includes the implant in the eye of a set of four square millimeters electrodes that stimulate the optic nerve. Once the signals reach the brain, the patient can see again.

The importance of medicine in applications of AI has been truly remarkable, to the extent that these applications have their own name: AIM, an acronym of AI in medicine that, for 15 years, has evolved as an active and growing discipline.

While the first applications of AIM have been, especially diagnosis and treatment have emerged with greater force other applications of AI in the medical and pharmaceutical sector: optimal resource management, staff scheduling, forecasting needs to help organic chemistry analysis and management of scientific information, which have contributed more or Casiones profitability problems mentioned diagnosis.

In the field of diagnosis and treatment, AI has important achievements: MYC 1976 in Stanford, infectious disease; CASNET 1979 at Rutgers, ophthalmology 4.5; INTERNIST 1980, Pitsburg, internal medicine; PIP 1971, MIT, on kidney disease; Al/Rheum 1983, at the University of Missouri, on diagnosis in rheumatology, SPE 1983; Rutgers, to interpret the results of electrophoresis of serum proteins produced by analytical instruments; TIA 1984, at the University of Maryland, on therapy of ischemic attacks.

To achieve this intelligent behavior different tools available. One is the mechanization of reasoning, binding statements or syllogisms; this concept of mechanical rationality, which is the origin of so-called expert systems, is really well before the advent of computers. In its history, we find the concept of systematic rationality of Descartes in "discourse on method" from 1637 and reasoning and symbolic calculus in Hobbes, in 1651, but until the advent of computers, these ideas do not materialize.

Medicine is another field in which are also using AI techniques. Scientific Research Institute in the US Human Genome and Lund University in Sweden have developed a technique that applies AI about chips that are beginning to be used for genetic analysis shows, called "biochips," and allowing them quickly distinguish between various types of cancer. Moreover, several teams of scientists are trying to create systems with a large number of geriatric diseases that cause memory loss. Power systems combine cognition AI software, GPS technology, infrared sensor networks, and nameplates accompanying the patient to all places. "With computer-assisted cognition,

Despite the advantages offered by AI, some people are against such provide "intelligence" to the machines. Physicist Stephen Hawking has warned of the urgent need to genetically improve the human species and prevent computers dominate the world. "Unlike our intellect," he says the physicist, "computers double their capacity every 18 months and there is a real danger that can create its own intelligence and take over." Another of its managers is to stimulate the development of technologies that enable direct communication between computers and humans, so that the machines contribute to humanity instead of rebelling against it.

With the passage of time man has developed different technologies to help human beings as was first with the invention of the wheel many years ago; today we managed to play impressive tasks that our ancestors never even thought that there is still much room to go and discover.

With the help of AI, we have been able to move faster on technology invented devices to perform tasks around us as well as develop systems to help human beings, perhaps changing a lack of technological prosthetic limbs. Through these inventions, technology has reached such a point created a fundamental and necessary part for our future and it is in the field of transportation, agriculture, architecture, medicine, biotechnology, and many more.

The care of children or even have technology such as artificial neural networks (ANN) to the point of never need to handle more, just tell where to take us and our transport that moves by itself with all the security. These are projects that man has had in mind already being put in place, all for the help of man and to return life easier.

AI has changed the course of human beings in every way and we cannot figure out where it will go because every time you find or develop something new always people are going to think of something even better, more compact, and more complex.

There are many projects to reach the point of returning to more machines than human nature; this can backfire because it may encourage many but some can take advantage of this and continue with crime and evil to destroy rather than help. But over time, they will reveal new technologies and projects as man's perspective is to achieve perfection.

8.2. CONCLUSIVE REMARKS

Will a thinking machine be able to relate mental content and refer to herself? Moreover, can it think rationally?

Yes, but not yet. We do not see a ban on the possibility of a strong AI, although we must warn the enormous difficulties facto that get in the way.

Fortunately, we cannot determine a priori the horizon as possible and punish the impossible. We do not know, really, what it is impossible for the human mind, beyond insurmountable logical inconsistencies (cannot think contradictory, for example).

Thus, a sum of prudence and confidence in the ability of human beings to transcend boundaries that seemed insurmountable should guide our research in these fields.

Right decisions are what make the difference, and therefore you need to seek appropriate measures to achieve the desired objectives tools. Implementing information storage helps to have a better view of events and at the same time gives support decision-making. In a competitive world like today, it is no longer possible to run out technology to support business management. Historical information and then plays a definite role in the course of business.

Understanding the business process is one of the primary activities that must be completed, to have a macro vision of the company so we can better define the key points that identify the strengths and weaknesses of a company.

It is recommended that when deploying information storage, a study was conducted to define how to manage resources and a strategy for updating the data load, depending on the type of business and the information you want to consult is established. In addition, it is vitally important to perform deployment with skilled and specialized people in the field, since a bad definition of procedures could result, unexpected output information.

Information storage success is not in its construction, but use it to improve business processes, operations, and decisions. In order for information storage to be used effectively, it requires understanding the impacts of implementation in different areas of the organization. When building storage information, it requires that persons involved, who will use the information, participate directly. Unlike application development, where requirements of the company manage to be relatively well-defined product stability business rules over time. Build information storage depends on the reality of the company and the conditions that exist at that time, which determine which should contain the information storage.

Regarding access to information storage, this is intended to provide data that enable users to access their own information when they need it. This approach used to provide information has several implications:

- People of the company may need to learn new skills.
- Extensive analysis and programming delays for information will

be deleted. As information is ready to be accessed, expectations are likely to increase.

- New opportunities may exist in the business community for information specialists.
- A large number of reports on paper will be reduced or eliminated.
- Information storage maturity will depend on the active use and feedback from its users.

Application usage support for decision-making by users of applications, require less expertise to build their own information and develop new skills. In conclusion, the value of information storage is described in three dimensions:

- **Improve the Delivery of Information:** complete, accurate, consistent, timely, and accessible information. Information that people need, in time, you need it, and in the format, you need.
- **Improve Decision Making Process:** With more support information obtained faster decisions; also, business people acquire greater confidence in their own decisions and those of the rest, and achieves a greater understanding of the impacts of their decisions.
- **Positive Impact on Business Process:** When people are given access to better quality information, the company can achieve alone:

– Eliminate delays business processes resulting from incorrect, inconsistent, and/or non-existent information.

– Integrate and optimize business processes through shared and integrated information sources use.

– Eliminate the production and processing of data that are not used or needed as a result of poorly designed or unused applications.

Bibliography

1. Ahmed, A. S. F., (2010). *The Important Characteristics to Make a Good Website*. Rochester Institute of Technology- New York, United States.
2. Alpaydin, E., (2009). *Introduction to Machine Learning*. Cambridge, MIT Press.
3. AS, & MG, (2014). *Universidad Tecnologica Nacional, Facultad Regional La Plata; La Plata, Buenos Aires, Argentina*. Retrieved from: http://www.frlp.utn.edu.ar/materias/info2/IS-Sistemas%20de%20 Informacion.pdf (Accessed on 13 December 2019).
4. Baars, B. J., (1988a). *A Cognitive Theory of Consciousness*. New York, Cambridge University Press.
5. Baars, J. B., (1988b). "Global workspace theory of consciousness: Toward a cognitive neuroscience of human experience." In: *Progress in Brain Research* (Vol. 150, pp. 45–53).
6. Badaro, S., Ibanez, L. J., & Omen, M. J., (2013). http://www.palermo.edu. Retrieved from: http://www.palermo.edu/ingenieria/pdf2014/13/CyT_13_24.pdf (Accessed on 13 December 2019).
7. Barba, A., (2001). *"Would it be Possible to Create Artificial Intelligence?"* Editorial Sun, SA de CV, Reforma.
8. Benedek, M., Jauk, E., Fink, A., Koschutnig, K., Reishofer, G., Ebner, F., & Neubauer, A. C., (2014). "To create or to recall? Neural mechanisms underlying the generation of creative new ideas." In: *Neuroimage* (Vol. 88, pp. 125–133).
9. Borland Software Corporation, (2002). *Web Application Developer's Guide*. Scotts Valley: Borland Software Corporation.
10. Central University of Ecuador, (2014). http://www.uce.edu.ec. Retrieved

from: http://www.uce.edu.ec/documents/22994/4862310/3.%20 Estructura%20Seguimiento%20interno.pdf (Accessed on 13 December 2019).

11. Chong, S., Liu, J., Myers, A. C., Qi, X., Vikram, K., Zheng, L., & Zheng, X., (2007). *Secure Web Applications via Automatic Partitioning.* Retrieved from: https://www.cs.cornell.edu/andru/papers/swift-sosp07.pdf (Accessed on 13 December 2019).
12. De Santos, D., Lorente, V., De la Paz, F., Cuadra, J. M., Álvarez-Sánchez, J. R., Fernández, E., & Ferrández, J. M. (2010). A client–server architecture for remotely controlling a robot using a closed-loop system with a biological neuroprocessor. *Robotics and Autonomous Systems*, *58*(12), 1223-1230.
13. Dehaene, S., Changeux, J. P., Naccache, L., Sackur, J., & Sergent, C., (2006). "Conscious, preconscious, and subliminal processing: A testable taxonomy." In: *Trends in Cognitive Sciences* (Vol. 10, pp. 204–211).
14. Dehaene, S., Lau, H., & Kouider, S., (2017). "What is consciousness, and have it could machines?" In: *Science* (Vol. 358, pp. 486–492).
15. Engin, G., Aksoyer, B., Avdagic, M., Bozanli, D., Hanay, U., Maden, D., & Ertek, G., (2014). Rule-based expert systems for supporting university students. *Proceeded Computer Science*, 22, 23.
16. Ferri, B. F., (2004). *"The Numerous Problems of Artificial Intelligence."* EPSYS Yearbook.
17. Finkelstein, A. C., Savigni, A., Kappel, G., Retsehitzegger, W., Kimmerstorfer, E., Schwinger, W., & Feichtner, C., (2004). *Ubiquitous Web Application Development – A Framework for Understanding.* Retrieved from: http://www0.cs.ucl.ac.uk/staff/A.Finkelstein/papers/uwa.pdf (Accessed on 13 December 2019).
18. Friston, K., (2018). "A theory of cortical responses." In: *Philosophical Transactions of the Royal Society of London B: Biological Sciences* (Vol. 360, pp. 815–836).
19. Fuster, J. M., (2013). *The Neuroscience of Freedom and Creativity: Our Predictive Brain*. New York, Cambridge University Press.
20. Gellersen, H. W., & Gaedke, M., (1999). *Internet Computing*. IEEE.
21. Hastie, T., Tibshirani, R., & Friedman, J., (2009). "Unsupervised learning." In: *The Elements of Statistical Learning* (pp. 485–585).

22. Horn, R. V., (1993). *Statistical Indicators for the Economic and Social Sciences*. Hong Kong.
23. http://www.fgcsic.es/lychnos/es_es/articulos/inteligencia_artificial (Accessed on 13 December 2019).
24. ISO, (2008). *ISO 9001: Quality Management Systems – Requirements*. Switzerland.
25. Skapura, D. M. (1996). *Building neural networks*. Addison-Wesley Professional.
26. Kurose, J. F., & Ross, K. W., (2009). *Computer Networking: A Top-Down Approach* (5th edn.). Boston: Pearson.
27. Lazhoz-Beltra, R., (2004). "*Bioinformatics: Simulation, Artificial Life and Artificial Intelligence*." Ediciones Díaz de Santos, SA, Madrid.
28. Luis, G. F., (2004). "Use and applications of artificial intelligence." *Science and Man, 3*(XVII).
29. Luján, M. S., (2002). *Web Application Programming: History, Basic Principles and Web Clients*. Alicante: University Club.
30. Merzenich, M. M., Recanzone, G., Jenkins, W. M., Allard, T. T., & Knot, R. J., (1988). "Cortical plasticity representational." In: *Neurobiology of Neocortex* (pp. 41–67).
31. Mondragón, P. A. R., (2002). *University Pablo de Olavide*. Retrieved from: http://www.upo.es/ghf/giest/ODTA/documentos/Indicadores/mondragon_indicadores.pdf (Accessed on 13 December 2019).
32. *Moodle*, (2015). Retrieved from: https://moodle.org/ (Accessed on 13 December 2019).
33. Moriello, S. A., (2004). "*Physical Agents Autonomous Develop: Can Roller Genuine Behavior?*" Master's Book. Master's degree in engineering information system.
34. NAC, National Accreditation Commission, (2007). *General Evaluation Criteria for Professional Careers*. Santiago.
35. *National University of Colombia*, (2003). Retrieved from: http://diracademica.manizales.unal.edu.co/index.php/procesos-liderados/sistema-de-informacion-academica-sia (Accessed on 13 December 2019).
36. O'Brien, J. A., & Marakas, G. M., (2009). *Introduction to Information Systems Fifteenth Edition*. New York: McGraw-Hill/Irwin.

37. Pearsonhighered, (2014). *Web Application Basics*. Retrieved from: http://www.pearsonhighered.com/samplechapter/0201730383.pdf (Accessed on 13 December 2019).
38. Penrose, R., (1991). *"The Emperor's New Mind* (p. 42)." Barcelona: Grijaldo, Mundari.
39. *Proemsa*, (2014). Retrieved from: http://www.proemsasoftware.com/software-gestion-academica-para-universidades/ (Accessed on 13 December 2019).
40. Quintana, T. L., (2007). *Expert Systems and Applications*. Hidalgo, Mexico: Universidad Autonoma del Estado de Hidalgo.
41. RAE, (2015). *Royal Spanish Academy*. Retrieved from: http://lema.rae.es/drae/?val=multiplataforma (Accessed on 13 December 2019).
42. Rodriguez, R. J. M., & Daureo, C. M. J., (2003). *Information Systems: Technical and Legal Aspects*. Almeria.
43. Roth, E. M., Bennett, K. B., & Woods, D. D. (1987). Human interaction with an "intelligent" machine. *international Journal of Man-machine Studies*, *27*(5-6), 479-525.
44. Searle, J., (1980a). "Minds, brains and science." Behavioral and brain. *Sciences, 3*, 417–424.
45. Shipsey, R., (2010). http://www.londoninternational.ac.uk/. Recovered from: http://www.londoninternational.ac.uk/sites/default/files/computing-samples/co1108_ch1–3.pdf (Accessed on 13 December 2019).
46. Shklar, L., & Rosen, R., (2003). *Web Application Architecture*. Chichester: John Wiley & Sons.
47. *SINAI*, (2013). Retrieved from: http://www.sinai.net.co/Web/Sinai/QueEs.aspx (Accessed on 13 December 2019).
48. Sotolongo-Aguilar, G., Guzmán-Sánchez, M. V., Saavedra-Fernández, O., & Carrillo-Calvet, H. A. (2001). Mining informetric data with self-organizing maps. *M Davis, CS Wilson, eds*, *8*, 665-673.
49. Stair, R., & Reynolds, G., (2012). *Fundamentals of Information Systems*. Boston, USA: Course Technology, Cengage Learning.
50. Stuart, R., & Peter, N., (2004). *"Artificial Intelligence."* A Mod-Erno Approach 'Pearson Education. SA, Madrid.
51. Tarafdar, M., & Zhang, J., (2005–2006). Analysis of critical website characteristics: A cross-category study of successful websites. *Journal*

of Computer Information Systems, 24.

52. Torres, L. Q., (2003). "Essays on automatic: Its definition: Theoretical extension of its applications." In: *Limbo: Bulletin of Studies on Santayana* (Vol. 17, pp. 11–13).
53. Turing, A. M., (1950). "Computing machinery and intelligence." *Mind, 43*, 433–460.
54. United Nations (UN), (1999). *United Nations*. Retrieved from: http://www.un.org/documents/ecosoc/docs/1999/e1999–11 (Accessed on 13 December 2019).
55. Valacich, J., & Schneider, C., (2011). *Information Systems Today Managing in the Digital World*. New Jersey: Pearson.
56. Wendy, R. H. B., (1985). *"Applications of Artificial Intelligence in Business, Science and Industry."* Prentice-Hall, Inc.
57. White, C., (2018). *Integration of Knowledge*. in Spanish, Madrid, Evohé.
58. White-Pérez, C. C., (2018a). "Competition, cooperation, and the mechanisms of mental activity." In: *Frontiers in Psychology* (Vol. 9, p. 1352).
59. White-Pérez, C., (2018b). "The logic of creativity." In: *The Heythrop Journal* (Vol. 59, pp. 1–19).
60. Yamasato, E. C., (2006). *Ministry of Education of the Government of Peru*. Retrieved from: http://www.minedu.gob.pe/planificacionestrategica/xtras/SubsistemaSAEvPlanes.pdf (Accessed on 13 December 2019).
61. Zeki, S., & Shipp, S., (1988). "The functional logic of cortical connections." In: *Nature* (Vol. 335, p. 311).

INDEX

Printed in the United States
By Bookmasters